Why Was I Born?

SECOND EDITION

What is my purpose for being here?
A Humanistic View of life

By Lyle L Simpson

The Humanist Press
Washington, DC

First printing © 2005

Second Edition © 2011

ISBN 978-0-931779-02-2

Published By
The Humanist Press
American Humanist Association

1777 T Street
Washington, DC 20009-7125

Our society frequently utilizes religious invocations at the beginning of organizational meetings. Even humanists are called upon to contribute to this effort to sanctify a meeting. Following is a humanist version of a public meditation that can be used for such purpose:

A Humanist Meditation

As we look to those forces of our universe that are beyond our current understanding that many collectively reverently call God, may we tune ourselves to reality, accepting what we cannot change, but changing what we may, in order that we may maximize the use of our talents and resources, while minimizing the conflicting motives of others, in our efforts to actualize our own lives, and thereby increase our own happiness and that of those that we love, in our endeavors to make our own lives significant by making our world a better place because we have lived our own life here on Earth today.

Lyle L. Simpson

Preface

Lyle L. Simpson is an attorney practicing law in the Midwest, with a humanistic practice. He specializes in the positive side of law by helping his clients create whatever is important in their lives. This includes forming their business entity from the origin of an idea through whatever makes them successful. He helps his clients through succession planning, to maximize the value of what they have created during their lifetime, and estate planning necessary to make the greatest statement of the meaning of their own lives.

Mr. Simpson's undergraduate degree, in psychology and philosophy, was supplemented with significant post-graduate work in both fields of study. He has been a member of the American Society of Humanistic Psychologists. He has lectured extensively on the philosophy of humanism and the psychology of Dr. Abraham Maslow.

Mr. Simpson served for five years as President of the American Humanist Association, and has also served as General Counsel of the Association for over thirty-five years. He served one year as Chairman of the Board to assist his successor, Isaac Asimov, to serve as President of the AHA. He created and is currently President of The Humanist Foundation, which he formed to assure preservation of his philosophy of life for future generations.

Mr. Simpson became intrigued with the study of ancient history and its profound effect upon our contemporary thinking. He is interested in biblical archeology, has attended numerous lectures, studied the Dead Sea Scrolls, and visited the site of Qumran in the West Bank of Israel where the scrolls were written, as well as the Shrine of the Book where they are currently preserved and are publicly displayed in Jerusalem.

These records from antiquity, known as the Dead Sea Scrolls, were written from about 250 BC through 67 AD. They remained hidden in caves until they were discovered in 1947. One lesson that they tell us is that our current religious traditions have been molded by history. Because we now find that many of our traditional assumptions regarding our purpose on Earth are not "immutable truths," this raises the question: Upon what authority do we base our very existence? "Why Was I Born?" is a question we must all answer for ourselves.

This essay was the last lecture of a series concerning the lessons we have learned from the Dead Sea Scrolls, which was delivered by the author to The Ray Society of Drake University in 2005. (Members are college graduates and alumni who return to campus to attend mini-university classes in order that they may continue their education, especially after their retirement.)

For many within our society their religious faith has become substantially threatened with the disclosure of recent archeological discoveries in the West Bank of Israel. Long held premises upon which their religious belief has been based may no longer be held as indisputable truths.

Because the faith of many in our society is threatened with the disclosure that the historic facts upon which their religious faith has been based may no longer be true, this lecture was contrasted with a lecture on the Islam religion, which is totally faith based. This lecture was intended to provide an alternative view of life that does not require faith. Those attending could then see a continuum of beliefs in order to contrast with their beliefs so that they could better understand for themselves where their traditions differ, and what religious traditions they personally value, and thereby be better able to reaffirm their own religious perspective.

This lecture was intended to give a view of life that is based solely upon our known truths, as validated by our scientific method of learning about our world. One of the basic tenets of humanism is that our knowledge is only tentative. As truth unfolds through discovery and research, generally using the scientific method, our beliefs and religious views should also grow and continually adapt to the changing world in which we live.

If you were raised on a deserted island, without authorities telling you what you should believe, an intelligent person could naturally acquire the philosophy of humanism. This is because when you view life without the influence of any outside authorities you only have nature to guide you.

Humanism does not require faith in order for our own lives to have purpose and for us to be able to live a good life. Humanism does not intend to challenge anyone else's faith, but humanists do affirm that people can live a good life based exclusively upon current empirical knowledge without a need for ascertaining our own truths by having to rely upon blind faith, or to base our life on Earth in the search for a life after death that may not exist.

What distinguishes humanists from many philosophies is the means humanists use to find acceptable truths. Some say that we have four distinct means of ascertaining truth. The first of these may be seen in the way we test the question of guilt or innocence in criminal trials through a Socratic method of debate. Two attorneys taking opposing positions test the veracity of the available evidence, and from this effort a decision maker in the form of a judge or jury determines the truth. This is the best system that we have for protecting the rights of an innocent defendant, but the system is hardly perfect. A humanist would not depend upon this means of ascertaining an immutable truth upon which they would be willing to base their existence on Earth.

The second means is evidenced by how some people are willing to rely upon authorities to establish what is true for themselves. Humanists may accept an authority tentatively, but would not rely upon them without question. To the degree that a proposition has importance in their lives humanists may accept it until a better answer appears, but they will want to continually test the veracity of that position.

A humanist is apt to be a skeptic. Most humanists cannot accept anyone's opinion, or any written word, as an ultimate truth upon which they would be willing to base their entire existence. At best, claims might be accepted tentatively, and then subject to continual testing against what they know to be true and that which is observable in our world.

Most authorities are eventually proven not to be the absolute truth. They are only the best current interpretation or analysis available, because our knowledge continually expands. Thus, accepting the opinion of another person or any text as an immutable truth on any subject is very difficult for a humanist.

Logic is the third technique for determining truth. Humanists are most apt to apply logic by applying their prior knowledge to any situation to ascertain the truth of a new proposition. They must be able to logically deduce the resulting truth by thinking through each step from truths that they already have validated, to arrive at a reasonable (and even then only tentative) acceptance of any new proposition. Our knowledge is continually subject to change with new information.

However, not all truths are discernible by deduction. The fourth means for ascertaining truths that humanists find most reliable are those arrived at through the scientific method. In science the researcher starts by observing or considering certain phenomena or events, establishing a hypothesis of what caused that occurrence, then testing their hypothesis to determine if it holds up as a plausible explanation of the phenomena. In order to be regarded as a valid theory other scientists must be able to duplicate the results before that hypothesis is accepted as true. Even then, the hypothesis is accepted only tentatively, and other scientists will continually test the theory, attempting to discredit or to improve upon it as more evidence comes to light. A humanist is most apt to accept this means of establishing what they will believe as reliably true. However, even these truths are always tentative.

Even though humanists are found in most religions, most humanists will not accept a particular religious doctrine or authority as an immutable truth based purely on faith. Most humanists will not do so even tentatively, especially as the sole basis for how they must live their lives. Since we have no evidence other than authorities for validating many religious notions, humanists generally would not accept the edict of any authority that claims that failure to accept their particular belief on faith would result in eternal damnation. No one knows the answer to such questions unequivocally and absolutely. We can only claim that we do; and history has shown that such claims are ultimately proven to be false.

Humanists may well participate within any particular religious tradition, but they would retain the freedom to doubt. Furthermore, they would usually view the relationship as only tentatively filling the gap in their search for answers to those questions we are capable of raising as we live our lives, for which science currently provides no clear answer. This is the approach taken in this endeavor to answer the question of "Why was I born?"

WHY Was I Born?

By Lyle L Simpson

*Does a flower blooming in an uninhabited wood have no value?
Has its life no purpose? Fulfilling its own destiny, in addition
to pollinating its posterity, may be its only purpose, but for that
flower, being the best that it can be is enough for its own life to
have meaning.*

Through the Hubble telescope astronomers have now discovered hundreds of thousands of galaxies, each with millions of stars. Carl Sagan, a popular humanist astronomer, once said to me, "In the known universe there are at least 300,000 planets, each of which is capable of sustaining life similar to that here on Earth." Therefore, he asserted, "It is rather vain of us to assume humans are the highest form of life in the universe." If there are higher forms of life, is our goal as humans to evolve into that form? That may be true, but what implications does not being the highest form of life have for why we are living our own life here on Earth today? *Why was I born?*

Donald Johansson, the paleoanthropologist who discovered "Lucy" (the evolutionary link which connects human existence from the amoeba to the ape), claimed that Lucy proves human existence to be an accident—an anomaly. Much like the arm on a Saguaro cactus is caused by a break in its surface; human existence appears to have occurred due to a breakdown in normal genetic evolution. Responding to my comments about Sagan's observation, Johansson pointed out that the statistical odds of such an anomaly occurring again are about 1 in 2 million. In a known population of only 300,000 planets, a second occurrence would be quite rare. Therefore, maybe we are the highest form of life in the universe. If humans are the highest life form in the Universe, does that provide "special meaning" for our own lives? Perhaps it would.

Most people wonder why he or she exists at some time in his or her life. In our early formative stage, others have attempted to answer that question for us. We accept their notions, at least initially, especially if they are our parent's view; and these experiences permanently influence our beliefs for the rest of our lives. We then often perpetuate those answers by passing them down to our children. After all, the purpose of our own existence is a difficult question to answer all by ourselves. Unfortunately, most of these answers are not well founded.

We are riddled with inconsistencies in our understanding of our world; and any evidence-based knowledge of why we are here on Earth today is still in its infancy.

There are many questions about our world that science has yet to answer. For instance, when asked if "God" exists, some have quoted today's "Einstein," Stephen Hawking, who has stated that, in viewing the basic forces of the universe in a unified theory, there is a gap that so far has only been explained as the presence of nature. Some may believe that this force is God.

Even though Hawking may not be religious in the traditional sense, he does share an awe of nature. Hawking's view does not necessarily imply a concept of an intelligent god micromanaging the universe in some supernatural fashion. He merely claims that, so far, we cannot understand some forces in the universe. We cannot, therefore, base a useful existence on Earth through guidance from such an impersonal god—other than to assume that we are supposed to live our lives in harmony with nature. We should already know that. Failure to live in harmony with nature is dangerous to our health.

But, Why Am I Here?

In *Spirituality Without Faith*, (*Humanist* magazine, January 2002), Thomas Clark reports that current science shows us that the universe is expanding, but does not have sufficient mass to collapse into another "Big Bang." He claims that ultimately all matter will turn to dust; the universe will become black and cold. Science shows that, apparently, our ultimate destiny is to become space dust—which does not make the issue of immortality very appealing. Perhaps it is not very realistic.

In *Whence Comes Death* (Ibid.), Joshua Mitteldorf discusses why humans die. We know that our bodies develop from a single cell that subdivides according to a unique genetic plan, creating all parts of our body. And, beyond that, at least every seven years, all cells in the body replace themselves. Apparently, there is no biological reason why we could not exist forever—or at least until our sun stops shining.

Mitteldorf points out that our physical aging deterioration is due to nature's evolution of the gene pool. As individuals we become irrelevant after our childbearing days. Therefore our genes contain a self-destruct mechanism to extinguish our existence in order to keep the gene pool evolving. If every human lived on Earth forever, the gene pool would never change. Apparently the purpose of human life is tied to the survival of the species, and not the individual. However, even this will become irrelevant when all earthly life becomes space dust. An ultimate purpose, or meaning, for our own existence remains unanswered. The truth is there might not be one.

Some people do not accept science as relevant in their view of life. Some assert, "Humans are merely living out God's plan." Yes, this notion answers the question simply and definitely—but it makes humans into puppets. If the script for our life is already written, why bother to live? Likewise, some believe in reincarnation, where we live successive lives until we ultimately become perfect. Unfounded as such a belief is, one can understand why those who find their life inadequate would welcome a chance to come back and try again. Unfortunately, few, if any, of these theories can survive informed intellectual scrutiny, and beyond that many people are simply unwilling to live their life based upon such unrealistic or trite premises. So surely there must be a better answer.

When we consider ourselves against the vastness of time and the universe, our individual existence becomes fairly insignificant. Why would any god even want to micromanage a tentative and all too short-lived speck on Earth? What would be the point?

Yet each of us has "faith" in something, even if it is only in the power of nature to respond to our actions. Such is the case when we correctly plant a seed. We have faith that nature will cause it to grow. My action was to plant the seed. We do not know why it grows, even though science can tell us how it grows. What happens after planting the seed is beyond my control, although I may continue to influence the result by watering the plant. However, nature may not really care whether that particular seed lives or dies. After all, it has plenty of others. Nature only provides the opportunity.

We soon learn that, as individuals, we are part of something that is bigger and more powerful than we are. The problem is that our ultimate relationship with our universe eludes us. Many more people today are content to believe that nature does not have to be fully understood for us to accept nature as being all that exists. Humanists are among them, and most humanists are willing to accept that such belief leaves many unanswered questions. Nature is really all that is available for us to interpret, and thereby understand, our own existence. Science is still expanding, and we are still learning.

However, some people expect more immediate completed answers, and left with few alternatives, they frequently fill in the gaps of verifiable knowledge with historically accepted religious answers from more primitive times, or they may even create answers of their own. Once any answer is accepted, no one likes to have his or her own answers challenged. Each of us feels that our own answer is "right" and, therefore, sufficient for ourselves. Thus, for some people requiring their "truth" to be based upon fact becomes irrelevant. These people frequently accept a myth as their own personal truth, and, once accepted, they will defend it until their death.

What is "Truth" For Me?

At the root of our ability to accept any belief for ourselves is how we determine what is true. Obviously, we cannot test every fact before accepting it as true for our own use—at least for that moment. For many of our beliefs we accept the opinion of people we trust.

Early in our lives we rely upon our parents, older siblings, teachers, and caregivers, for the answers to our questions. This is especially true when we are given answers to questions that we did not ask, such as the foundation for our religions views. We accept these answers for emotional reasons. At that moment truth is irrelevant.

As we mature, for those who are braver, some will test selected beliefs. But, even the brave will continue to accept some answers from others where they have no immediate personal concern for the answers.

Allowing authority figures to provide our answers is easier, and most people follow the path of least resistance. However, for those who are less prone to blindly accept the answers of others, they must be able to obtain the same results for themselves by testing at least some of their beliefs before then accepting them as their "truth."

Science is built on the principal of testing beliefs. For every observation of phenomena, scientists propose a hypothesis as an explanation. To be accepted as true by scientists, others must be able to test the theory by duplicating the result. If others are able to do so, the hypothesis is tentatively accepted as true until another answer emerges as a new hypothesis, usually based on a deeper level of explanation for the origins of those facts, and the process of our "truths" evolve to a deeper more informed level of belief.

For those living primarily on lower levels of intellectual growth, accepting childhood authorities in established religious faith beliefs may be sufficient for the rest of their lives. Others, especially those capable of living on higher psychological levels, may become skeptical. They may feel that more proof is necessary for something to be accepted as proven to them. Like scientists, many skeptics recognize that there are no absolute truths. All beliefs should be accepted tentatively. A notion may be accepted as tentatively true because it serves the moment, even though we may recognize that belief may not be relied upon as an absolutely indisputable "truth."

Many scientists apply the same standard to accepting their religious views that they apply to accepting observations of our physical world. Other scientists, and many other people, may accept their religious views as a matter of social or family convenience, and are, therefore, not troubled with testing the truth of their personal religious views.

Many people, however, are unable to accept any truth merely on "faith" that their authority is right; or by accepting that a "wish" that something may be true is tantamount to knowing that it is. Some people need to know for sure before accepting an important belief as an immutable truth. Humanists tend to be among them. To accept something as "true" most humanists must be able to test the facts for themselves. If they cannot prove it, they will not rely upon it. An untested belief is simply a wish that a skeptic recognizes may only be accepted tentatively. It does not matter to skeptics if the belief is a scientific theory or their religious beliefs.

Many people cannot accept uncertainty. When knowledge fails us, for the many people who fill the gap with myth or lore, it is difficult to base our existence on the notion that we are here only because nature merely allowed us to be—or, more specifically, that we are here as individuals only by the luck of the draw—although that probably is true. We each want to have a purpose for our own existence.

In our search for the meaning of life, what do we really know? Philosopher René Descartes probably stated it best when he said, essentially, *"I think, therefore, I am."* All anyone really knows for sure is that we, as individuals, momentarily exist. Every other belief we accept on some level of faith.

So What Does This Mean?

The more relevant question remains: *if all we know is that we exist, how do we establish purpose in our own life?* If our ultimate purpose is only the survival and growth of our species, is our reason for being here really only to procreate and then die like some male ant or black widow spider? If so, we older folks might as well get about our duty, and quit wasting Earth's resources. This is not a very satisfying thought.

We should at least have an answer to the question for ourselves. Human existence may have been an accident, as Donald Johansson suggests. A supernatural god may not be dictating our behavior. Yet this does not mean that, while we are here, our own life should not have value, at least for ourselves. The field of psychology may be the only currently available science that we can employ to increase our understanding of what is ultimately important in our own life.

Maslow's Purpose for Our lives

Dr. Abraham Maslow, the founder of humanistic psychology, has articulated a viable scientific theory for finding purpose in each individual life. Maslow recognized that there are several distinctly different levels, or categories, of human needs.

Maslow found that humans live on multiple psychological levels, and that our behavior, and our individual orientation to life, varies significantly depending upon which level we are primarily living on at the moment. Our current predominant need level regulates our momentary existence. Maslow believed that our objective in life is to achieve our own fulfillment by obtaining the highest level we are each capable of attaining. Maslow recognized that the meaning of fulfillment varies on each need level.

Psychology as a Science

Psychology originated as a science with Sigmund Freud. Freud assisted the mentally ill, to improve their lives by focusing on what was wrong with their behavior. Thus, psychology started as a negative science.

"Behaviorists" represent the second phase of psychology. Everyone has heard of Pavlov's dog that associated the ringing of a bell with the delivery of food. This proved that behavior could be conditioned.

B. F. Skinner, another humanist psychologist, built mazes in which he experimented with white rats, showing that they have the capacity to learn. Behaviorism shows that need deprivation causes drive, which results in behavior. By modifying any antecedent stimulus, behavior can be changed.

While I was studying in Drake University's Department of Behavioral Psychology, I was once told that we could toilet train a child in a day using a cattle prod. (Of course, the child would become neurotic for life, but the child's behavior certainly could be modified.)

Maslow grew up in this era. In an attempt to discern why two of his psychology professors were such wonderful people, Maslow could not ascertain what need deprivation caused their behavior. All of a sudden he realized that maybe psychology had the notion of "needs" backwards. When need deprivation is present, people become abnormal—until they eventually become sick, like Freud's patients. But when people are totally healthy, Maslow discovered, they lack need deprivation.

Maslow's Hierarchy of Needs

Maslow found that needs could be categorized by the strength of the drive level caused by their deficiency; and that needs with greater drive strength prevail. If a person is sufficiently hungry, for example, his or her behavior will address this issue first, deferring a wish to help others, or continuing to listen to classical music. Maslow found that there are six distinct hierarchical levels of human needs.

Survival is the primary concern of all living organisms. Hence it follows that the strongest, or primary, needs are those with physiological necessity. Included in these basic needs are the requirement for food, water, air, shelter, sex, elimination, warmth, and sleep, among others. If one really has to go to the bathroom, nothing else is particularly important at the moment. For purposes of illustration, these "basic needs" may be characterized as those needs with a strength level of one.

Once our essential basic needs are sufficiently attended, we naturally "feather our nests" to assure their future satisfaction. We become protective. Maslow classified this next level as "security needs," and found these needs typically have a strength level of less than one-half that of basic needs.

When we feel secure we will normally not think about the proximity of the closest bathroom. When we are unable to relieve ourselves, however, we certainly will worry about what happens the next time, especially if any barriers to our instant relief are present. A private in the Army having to go to the bathroom while standing at attention in formation learns that lesson very well. It never happens again.

Once secure, we naturally tend to seek friendships and love relationships—on the "social or belonging" need level. We want to belong and be accepted, and to be loved. We then bring others within our defense mechanisms and allow them to share the satisfaction of our needs. Although this is very important to all of us, these social needs have a deficiency strength level of approximately only one fourth that of our basic needs (try explaining that concept to a teenager with hormones).

When those we love and for whom we feel responsible are also safe, we are then able to feel that our lower level survival needs are reasonably satisfied. As a result, we are then free to seek recognition from others. Maslow classified this level as "ego, or esteem needs." Though ego strength can appear strong, the drive strength of these needs is typically only one-eighth that of basic needs.

Once we are satisfied that we are not only accepted, but appreciated, we are then free to identify with our environment. We then can recognize and become "in tune" with our own reality. Only then are we capable of actualizing our own existence and becoming a whole person.

Maslow defined "actualization" needs with fifteen different adjectives. They are: truth, goodness, beauty, unity, aliveness, uniqueness, perfection and necessity, completion, self-sufficiency, justice and order, simplicity, richness, effortlessness, playfulness, and meaningfulness.

When we are savoring the world around us we are attempting to fulfill the actualized level of our own needs. Yet, again, we are capable of achieving this goal only when our basic, security, social, and ego needs are reasonably satisfied.

Up to the point of actualization, Maslow recognized that our needs are deficit needs. If we have a deficit, we feel a need. Our behavior is essentially driven by the need for our own survival. Maslow said that these needs are "instinctoid" – instinct like needs. Actualization needs move into the realm of "being" needs. You strive to become the most complete, the fullest "self," hence the term Maslow used, "self-actualization." All creatures are totally selfish on the lower levels of living. Altruism only appears as we approach actualization.

What happens once we fully actualize our own existence is the most important of Maslow's discoveries. When we actualize our full potential, we may momentarily reach the state of total fulfillment. In this state of contentment we are able to resonate in harmony with our own environment. For at least that moment, we are free of all stress and may then recognize our own sense of peace as a *peak experience*." More than in any other prior experience in our lives, we feel truly exhilarated, liberated, and fulfilled in a peak experience.

However, even those who have actualized their own existence must spend most of their lifetime tending to lower level needs in order to be able to momentarily live on their highest level of living. We live predominantly on only one level at a time. Maslow found that our objective for life, living only within ourselves, is for our own continual growth and to sustain our life on the highest level we can attain.

Maslow discovered that once a person has arrived at a peak experience, some people are then able to make a transition from their own more selfish motivation and direct efforts beyond themselves. People are then able to accept external motivation that transcends into a cause, or another person, or a commitment. It can possibly be to their own physical detriment.

This allows their own lives to become even more significant and, thereby, ultimately even more meaningful to themselves. At that point we transcend our own self, and, in effect, become, in essence, "transhuman," feeling fully alive and in tune with all that surrounds us.

This sixth, or highest, level opens a new realm for living. A mother becomes one with her son or daughter; an artist becomes lost in his or her painting to the exclusion of eating and sleeping; a doctor works to save the patient he or she is serving to the point of a risk for his or her own peril; and a teacher may lose his or her own identity and becomes fully invested in his or her students.

A person currently living on this level has fused the needs of the people he or she serves, or of a cause or an idea, with himself or herself, and thereby those external needs may dictate his or her own needs and wants—even to the exclusion of that person's own personal needs.

A test to determine if a person is capable of living on this level is to analyze how they describe their own efforts. Does their own description of their life's work include him or her? Questions to ask of such people are, "What gives you the most satisfaction, or reward in your life?" "What gives your life the most meaning?" The transpersonal values expressed by people who have transcended beyond their own needs tell us a lot about that person. Once a person is capable of living on this level, the self merges into the cause, which has then become the primary purpose for that person's own existence.

Maslow labeled the phenomena "being-cognition," or "B-values," meaning that person is able to identify the purpose for his or her own existence with something beyond himself or herself. The "cause" becomes that person's motivation to exist. He or she becomes indistinguishable from his or her cause. In the end, they are not only able to become a whole person with a meaningful purpose for their own self, but they then measure their own lives in terms of the good they create.

Individuals can transcend themselves at any level of the hierarchy of needs. However, unless a person has actualized himself or herself, their motivation is primarily selfish. Only a person who is totally fulfilled lacks a personal unselfish motive. Below that level degrees of selfishness are the primary influence of our behavior.

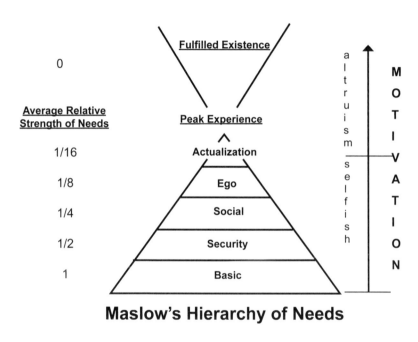

Maslow's Hierarchy of Needs

Ideally, people will earn their living doing whatever fulfills their own actualization and transcendent needs. For those able to do so, their mission in life provides a sense of purpose; thus, we may be capable of supporting all of our needs in life with work that fulfills our passion. Teachers, ministers, artists, doctors, even some lawyers and many other occupations may experience a sense of wellbeing and fulfillment, resulting from supporting all of their needs through their professional experience.

Maslow recognized that most people would probably never have a peak experience during their lives, let alone rise beyond that experience. Environment, or their own barriers, will prevent attaining fulfillment for their own lives. Most people will never even know that the opportunity for a higher level of living beyond their current existence is even available for them. That is unfortunate, but very true.

Our society must provide the opportunity for all if anyone is to ever succeed. However, providing the opportunity does not mean society should also give away the means. We must accept the responsibility, and produce the result for ourselves, for our own actualization to have any ultimate value.

Even though our society, for all intents and purposes, provides the opportunities for actualization of each life, most will still not succeed (even though people living in a free society have the freedom to do so). This is because actualization requires continual effort.

Like water running downstream, unmotivated behavior tends to follow the course of least resistance. Unless there is conscious effort applied by the individual to go against the current, real success cannot be achieved. For proof we only need to observe the success achieved by recent immigrants from oppressed societies who are now successfully living, and achieving, in our own country, and then contrast their behavior with that of those born here who expect to have what others have achieved, but are unwilling to do the work necessary to acquire their own success. The cultural contrast is vivid.

Taking advantage of opportunity takes initiative. You must really work for success. Lazy people do not have the anticipatory attitude that allows more successful people the exhilarating feeling they receive by moving toward a goal. Lazier people easily give up. Perhaps brutally stated, but those people who are provided opportunity, and are capable of succeeding but fail to exert themselves, deserve to live on a lower psychological level of life. No person is entitled to society providing more than the opportunity to achieve their own goals. You must earn the goal for yourself through your own effort.

Much like an athlete who feels good every time he or she performs a little bit better than the last time, most successful people can recognize a sense of reward by striving to attain their goals, even after expending only a little more effort. Success is the journey, not the result of reaching a goal. Once a goal is achieved a new goal should replace it in order that we can continue our own growth path. Attitude makes a huge difference in our ability to achieve success.

Even with a positive attitude, fulfillment must be earned by each of us if it is to have lasting value. Success breeds greater success. Attitude makes a difference. It has been previously said: "You are what you think you are," or "As you think, so you shall become." Attitude precedes your result.

Wishing to interview higher functioning people to better understand how they achieve fulfillment, and to understand the effect that peak experiences have in people's lives, Maslow first needed to know which ones were capable of actualizing their own existence. He first had to develop tests to find those who were living on the actualized level in order to identify people to interview.

His first test was music. Maslow found that a person living on the basic level found only strong and definite music—loud, hard rock or percussion—to be meaningful. Because we start our lives on the basic level, this may explain why our children prefer loud percussion music in the earlier part of their lives. Like all other aspects of life, unfortunately, some never grow out of it.

A person on the social level can easily appreciate popular music. In turn, on the actualized level, a person will be more apt to find subtle orchestrations, such as Beethoven, to be beautiful. A person on the actualized level could also appreciate hard rock, as well as the full range of music, though normally they may prefer more classical or subtle orchestration. However, the person living on the basic or security level will typically never enjoy Beethoven.

For another test Maslow used humor. For a person living on the basic or security level, violence, sex, or some other harsh event, must be included to be perceived as humor. On the social level, jokes about people may be perceived as funny. On the actualized level, incongruence could be humorous. Again, the person on the basic level will seldom understand why something incongruent could be funny, while a person on the actualized level could appreciate an "off-color" joke, as well as the greater range of humor. For a person living on the basic, or security level, the perception of abstraction in any form is seriously limited. Using these means of testing will help us differentiate the level of living of those we encounter and, therefore, better understand those with whom we must interact.

Satisfaction of each need is not linear, but rather a bell curve with a dimple, or "node," at the top. Pain can result both from deprivation as well as the excess satisfaction of a need. For instance, one may be thirsty, start drinking water, and feel significantly better until a peak is reached. From there, a little more water will cause a slight decent, until one feels totally satiated for thirst. Drinking more water will result in excess, at which time ultimately one will once again begin feeling pain. A person can die from either deprivation or from excess. The same path is true for all needs.

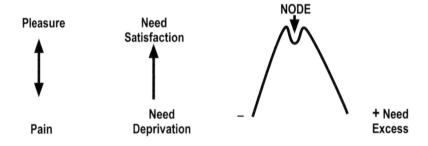

Homeostasis is the state of balance. It works much like the thermostat of your furnace; need more, it turns the heat on, need less, you get air-conditioning. The objective for the satisfaction of any need is to remain within the node, or balance point. Our objective in life is living a balanced existence with all of our needs reasonably satisfied. If, in fact, all of our needs at any given moment are fully satisfied, we can achieve the very unique condition where we are in harmony with our immediate environment. This state, which Maslow labeled a "peak experience," tells us that for that instant we are fully living on the highest level of our own existence. A fully satiated person enjoying a peak experience is resting within the node of all his or her needs.

When a peak experience occurs, much like a tuning fork, you resonate with your own reality. You are, for that brief moment, "in tune" with your own universe. It may be subtle, and could be missed. Or, you may experience a euphoric feeling—much like floating in air. While in this state you fully comprehend, and are comfortable with all aspects of life around you, even if you might otherwise be stuck in a negative situation. People in jail—even those having just filed for bankruptcy or in proceedings for a divorce—are still capable of achieving this state under the right circumstances. Obviously, it is more difficult if their attention is otherwise occupied. However, achieving fulfillment is conditioned by our attitude toward our current situation.

Many of us in our American culture and environment will have felt a peak experience from time to time without recognizing what was happening, or understanding its significance. Because at the moment of a peak experience everything in the world feels right, this can be very scary if one has no basis for understanding what is happening. Maslow believed that the typical "born-again experience" of an evangelical fundamentalist is probably a peak experience labeled in religious terms. It is an "ah, ha!" moment. Because some people are unable to articulate their experience in scientific terms, they will look to what they know to explain the phenomenon, and might, thereby, credit God with their own sense of wellbeing.

For the person on death row in prison, having a peak experience does not mean that they would approve of their incarceration. However, at that moment, they would at least understand their situation, and then be able to accept the inevitable. They will at least momentarily have much greater insight. A person dying of cancer similarly may have such an experience if he or she has become resigned to their fate. Hospice services do wonders in helping people accept their own deaths using this principle.

For Maslow, being able to achieve a peak experience is the "apex" of our own personal existence, fully living within our own selves. We become a totally "healthy" person, in a psychological sense. In doing so, we have, at that moment, fulfilled anything and everything that is relevant. We are then fully alive, and perfectly content.

Living on the actualized level with sustained peak experiences would be difficult, if not impossible. However, if we can capture this moment where we no longer have personal needs, we can then transcend beyond ourselves to become in tune with a cause, or a greater purpose. We then can become a fully functioning person, whose life is not only meaningful to our self, but upon transcending we become even more significant to others.

We must recognize that peak experiences are very subtle. The euphoric feeling may be intense, but there is no strong drive level within ourselves to cause behavior when we reach a peak experience. The experience will be momentary. Because a lower level need with stronger drive will soon take over—we inevitably become hungry, or face a call of nature—our behavior will change to fulfill this new need because of its higher drive strength.

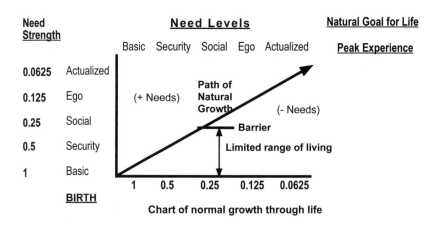

Chart of normal growth through life

Traveling the actual path of growth through life

Growth does not occur in a straight line. We experience periods of living on a flat plateau while fulfilling the needs on each level as we progress. Moving to the next level for the first time is dramatic. Similar to being a seedling on the basic level, and then becoming a plant on the security level, we continue to grow, and mature. Realizing that we have arrived on a higher level is as apparent as if you were a rose bud on the social level that blossoms into an *American Beauty*

Rose on the ego level. On the actualized level, our concerns may shift to perpetuating the opportunity to bloom for others.

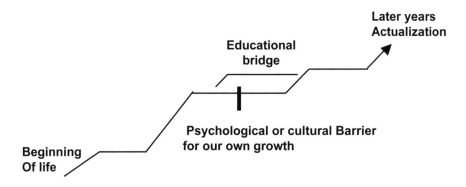

Typical successful growth path through life

To reach the next level we must be open and accessible for growth. As we age, higher growth can become more difficult because we have acquired more assets, or status, that requires protection, and we may have established artificial goals that absorb much of our energy. On the other hand, as we reach retirement, actualizing may become easier, because we no longer feel threatened, and we may no longer feel that we must impress others to get ahead in life.

If we must become "president" of the Junior League to become momentarily self-satisfied, we can hardly be expected to recognize other opportunities above the ego level. It is laudable to serve as president of such a worthy organization. The distinction is the level of need that motivated our desire to be president. Were we striving to be president for recognition, for the satisfaction of our own ego, or for the good that we can provide the world by leading such a worthy organization?

On the ego level and below we can absorb so many problems in daily living that we cannot truly appreciate life. Many of us have to reach retirement before we are able to release our sense of commitment to artificial goals, and we can then become free to accept new opportunity and growth in our lives.

Only if we are able to overcome our lower barriers in concert with our other needs being currently satisfied, are we capable of having the sensation that everything is, for at least that moment, "right" in our lives. According to Maslow, actualization is the state of existence that we all should seek, and at that moment we will be free of our own limitations. At that point we may be able to transcend our own selfish needs, allowing ourselves to magnify the good that we can accomplish in our life for others. That should be our goal if we truly wish to fulfill our own existence while we are here on Earth.

Why Is Achieving Actualization so Difficult?

We live in a world of violence. All life on Earth is prisoner to an environment where only the fittest survive. The first and primary goal of every person or life of any form—ranging from insects to the artificial life forms of government, business, and institutions—is the same. The primary goal of anything is to survive.

Change threatens existence. Preserving the status quo is every form of life or entities' constant effort. As we do so we affect the lives of others, sometimes negatively. The food chain dictates that weaker life forms sacrifice their own life in order that others higher in the chain survive—but this does not mean that they do so willingly. Those about to be devoured fight for their own existence. You only need to try fishing to understand this principle.

Humans are as much a part of the natural world as any other species; every person's environment on Earth frequently is cruel. We each learn to defend ourselves from pain from the day we are born. Our constant quest to live compels us to continually try to improve upon our existing condition in life. Since our own survival is essentially a basic need, we cannot easily do anything else. However, we cannot healthily grow on our own. We must interact with our environment and with others within our culture in order to survive. These outside factors condition our behavior.

The many techniques we create to protect ourselves from threats, especially those that are produced by outside forces, may cause barriers for our own continued growth. Such barriers can block our natural progression toward the actualization of our full potential. To circumvent such barriers, in order that we may continue normal growth along our natural path, requires continual conscious effort.

If we want to actualize our own life—to become truly healthy and able to transcend into a new realm of living—the first task requires recognition of where barriers exist. Seldom do we see our own barriers. People feel safer living within known parameters; and, therefore, many are content with their current existence. Indeed, removal of barriers requires more effort and risk than many are willing to endure. Most live without the knowledge that higher, more rewarding opportunities are even available to them.

It is an all too human tendency to follow the path of least resistance. Growth is not always easy. The character, Eliza Doolittle, spent the entire length of the movie, *My Fair Lady*, learning how to grow beyond her earlier life. Many are unwilling to expend the effort, and are content to remain within the confines of their reduced existence. They are, thereby, condemned to not ever being able to actualize their own existence. That is truly tragic.

To continue to grow, we must continuously concentrate on identifying, and then eliminating, barriers if we ever wish to become fulfilled, and to actualize our own existence. Barriers occur normally without our knowledge, or consent. All barriers need to be immediately challenged if they are to be easily eliminated. Left alone, barriers harden from temporary protections to become permanent fixtures. They become defense mechanisms that ultimately take over, thus limiting our range of behavior. In that manner barriers become a scotoma.

A "*scotoma*" is a blind spot in our own view of reality. Scotomas are immutable beliefs. Formal education may be the best means of addressing these concerns. Learning new information in a non-threatening environment can provide bridges over, or paths around, barriers, rather than hitting our beliefs head on where our own scotomas will resist change.

Forcing ourselves to reach a little further with each activity can do wonders to keep barriers from developing fixations in our own life, as well as in the lives of our children and significant others that we have allowed within our defense mechanisms.

Some barriers may be physical, such as limitations upon space, time, or available diet, while others may be belief systems. Some are caused by ill health, or our own previous failures; but more often they are caused by the culture in which we live.

As a seemingly innocent example, the Jewish population historically denied the faithful the right to eat pork because trichinosis was early in its history a serious problem. Even though this disease is not a significant problem today (at least in the United States), the restriction continues as tradition. Consequently, a Jewish person eating pork might feel guilty, thus denying him or her pleasure in that food. Like water running down hill, we take the easiest path. The easiest path for any of us is not to participate in any activity that causes stress, or discomfort.

Likewise, some within the Catholic faith may still feel it is a sin to eat red meat on Friday (at least during Lent), even though that tradition was largely created to support a declining fish industry. The tradition now takes on an entirely new symbolic meaning within the Catholic faith today. This is an example of how our religious views have evolved.

These examples are relatively unimportant, and if they have value for an individual, no one else should care. However, some irrational cultural restrictions can be harmful. A Christian Scientist denying a child essential medical care because of his or her personal religious beliefs may be one example. Yet it is easy to see how these limitations occur in society. Because all forms of irrational barriers prevail in our culture, finding better paths for living is fertile ground for those wishing to improve society.

Alternative Paths to Actualization

Our body is the "temple" of our own lives. It seems foolish not to protect it. The question may be asked, "If our goal is merely to reach a peak experience, why should we not shortcut the path by using drugs, or possibly alcohol?" Some drugs certainly could cut through all forms of barriers. But is the peak experience achieved with drugs genuine? You would never know.

The purpose for the barrier was to protect you from something. With drugs, an individual would have blasted right through their personal barriers. The experience could have serious negative psychological side effects—let alone the established fact that the drugs themselves could permanently harm your body. Therefore, drug use is not an acceptable path for actualization.

Fully living each step of one's own life seems to be the only acceptable path for genuine fulfillment of our own existence. There are no shortcuts for a quality life. Success is the journey, or our measure of the value of the path we have chosen, and not the ultimate goal. Once reached, each goal is replaced with a new one. It is our journey through life that should matter to us, at least while we are here. That is all that has true real value. Possessions accumulated, and titles acquired, ultimately mean little without the quality of life that we have been able to live. Achieving the highest level of living our own life that we are capable of attaining is all that truly matters.

How does my attitude make a difference?

Whether I have an open mind, conducive to learning, and therefore growth, or whether my mind is closed and I am content within my own world, is solely up to me. Attitude, indeed, makes the greatest difference. My attitude is the most critical element in determining the quality of my own life, and the effect that I have on others.

Some authorities declare that there is a "law of attraction" that acts like a magnet pulling our opportunities, or our defeats, out of the mass of stimuli that surrounds us daily. Like fixed ideas we have about certain brands of clothing, or foods, the mental orientation we have filters the receipt of all new information, determines its reception, and our interpretation of new data. We make decisions based upon our bias. Our attitude is the filter that defines how we react to the information that we currently receive.

The attitude that we project to others also influences the response that we receive from them. Even when we are alone, our own attitude becomes a self-fulfilling prophecy. We get back what we project and our attitude molds how we react to what we then receive. This creates a spiral effect that can either ascend to greater heights and opportunities, or our attitude reinforces negative feelings, causing our descent which may well lead to a state of unhappiness and chaos. More simply stated; a positive happy attitude must precede our actions if we wish to affect our ability to attain positive results.

By modifying our reception of new information we receive we modify its effect upon us. Our attitude will determine the effect new information will have on us. Adopting our current attitude is the primary daily control that we have over our life. By being receptive to new information we are able to grow and expand our view of life, and to accept change that can enhance our life.

If we do not intentionally choose our own attitude in any given moment, we are then subject only to fate. By keeping an open mind we are better able to challenge negative information and absorb beneficial information. If we are indifferent, the information that we next receive may be subject to the attitude we held for the preceding event. Instead of assuming responsibility for our lives, events will rule us.

We can only live in the present moment. Living in the past may give us a false sense of accomplishment, or a foreboding expectation of failure. That will not only influence our current attitudes and feelings about ourselves, but the result will distort reality. Ultimately, living in the past accomplishes nothing to improve our future except to provide us information in a primitive attempt to protect us from failure, or to create wishes that we may not be sufficiently motivated to achieve.

The past is only prelude. It can either influence our current attitude, or be ignored by us. That is our choice. The only aspect of our lives that we actually control is how we perceive and accept new data or stimulation that we are receiving at this very moment.

Our past experiences may enhance our ability to predict the outcome of our current situation, but the result is not inevitable. If an individual prefers a different result, the only way that they can influence the achievement of that result is by changing how they interpret their current situation. If you think positively toward an objective you are much more apt to have a positive result.

I like the statements "You are what you think that you are," or "As you think, so you shall become," and "Whether you think you can, or you can't, you're right."

Our opinions of ourselves in our current situation will more often than not, determine the outcome of our current behavior. It takes fate or luck to cause any other result. We should be unwilling to live our lives relying upon fate. If we truly want to live our own life, we must be the cause of whatever happens next.

Successful people enhance their opportunity to create successful results because successful people believe they will be successful. It all starts with attitude. They believe in themselves and know that they can achieve what they want to achieve. The opposite view is also true, and even more powerful. With a negative attitude you can become your own worst enemy.

If we approach our current situation expecting success, and encounter a momentary setback because the ball did not hit the basket, or an intervening event caused a different result than expected, we should view that event as a new opportunity to learn and proceed with greater enthusiasm. People who do not take charge of their own attitude will be more apt to curse the cause or their result, blame themselves, and feel badly that they "failed."

How we react will determine what happens next. Successful people see loss as momentary and an opportunity to learn so that they can deal with those factors differently next time. It is up to each individual as to how they will react. The only control we have over our life is our current attitude, and that will influence our future.

If we are afraid that we will lose the race, or the wrestling match, or miss the shot because we have not practiced, or because we missed it last time, or we weigh too much, or whatever, we have created the environment that will produce that result. Our attitude becomes our own self-fulfilling prophecy.

Some people pray for a result and then keep doing it with the next problem they face because it appeared to work before. However, it may well be because they have created a positive attitude toward achieving their objective, and not because God intervened in their life.

One resulting aspect of prayer is that it does tune oneself to reality. Those with a religious perspective may say, "God rewards those who believe." In contrast, when they lose or fail, some will not accept the responsibility by saying, "It was God's will."

Meditation is what is really working. God may have nothing to do with it. After all, it is terribly vain of us to actually believe that our own "God" will intervene to make a change in our lives that will affect the outcome of our behavior. The implication is that only we are special to God and our competitors are not. At best, the only thing we can say for sure is that we are affecting our own attitude by focusing on the result that we wish to obtain.

There are many ways to become in tune with oneself. Meditation works. It clears all other thoughts out of your mind and focuses on one thought at a time. By focusing on a thought we open our reception to that thought either negatively or positively depending upon our attitude at that moment. Psychology explains that it is our attitude that orients our lives and influences the result of our behavior by enhancing our expectations, energy, and drive toward an objective, or requiring us to reject it. Our current positive attitude allows us to focus upon the goal and to become more receptive to the subtle opportunities that will enhance the result we wish to achieve.

The opposite is also true. Consider the effect of the behavior of a parent who feels a lack of their own success and projects that attitude upon their own children. The parent then wonders why his or her child has low self-esteem that results in a lack of success and, in some cases, disciplinary problems. A totally different result is achieved for the child whose parents support and believe in their child's own ability to achieve. Your own attitude makes a difference in the lives of others.

If we want to achieve only good results, then we should not allow our self to think negatively about anything. To test this, we should try thinking only positively for a day and see how we then feel about ourselves and the world around us at the end of the day. Given time it will become a habit that will work wonders. It is exceedingly important to remember that our attitude means everything, as it influences the results we attain through living our own life striving to be the very best that we are able to achieve.

Who Am I?

Recognizing that we can be deceived by how our mind works is important in order to better understand how our opportunities to experience life can become seriously limited. Everyone is oriented to life based upon his or her own perceptions. Our experiences condition the way in which new information is received. In psychology, conditioned orientation (our own attitude or expectation for the receipt of new stimuli) is called a "preparatory set." A preparatory set establishes the framework for how new information is received. The same stimuli may be totally accepted by one person and totally rejected by another, depending upon their own pre-existing orientation.

Once a stimulus, notion, or position is accepted to the exclusion of all others, we may become fixated in our own belief. We may then feel that this is the only belief that is acceptable. When a notion becomes valued to the exclusion of all other information it becomes a scotoma that acts similarly to a computer spam blocker.

Scotomas block any information contrary to our present belief, whether it is beneficial or not. Scotomas are the point at which our ability to accept any contrary notion ceases, our minds become closed, and further dialogue is useless. We are thereafter conditioned to be blind to reality on that particular issue. Our scotoma becomes our own reality—regardless of whether it is right or wrong.

Scotomas do help us filter information so that we can receive useful consistent data, and reject the vast amount of useless bits of information constantly bombarding us. They also harm us by denying us any further acceptance of the truth. When we internalize or accept notions as true for ourselves, they can become valued even when they are inconsistent with our own best interests, or even if they may be recognized as totally false when viewed as a part of reality.

We all have scotomas because our life-long task is processing the vast amounts of stimuli we constantly receive so that we may select those beneficial to our own survival and reject those that could be harmful. Once we select a life-mate, for example, no other person should thereafter be as important. That scotoma is necessary to maintain a healthy marriage.

Our goal should be to continue growing, by identifying and eliminating negative barriers before they become scotomas. The healthy approach is to not allow such psychological tools to become permanent barriers for growth. By recognizing how our experiences can combine to create unfounded expectations, we can reduce many of the barriers we encounter to our growth. An example of how our mind works may be helpful for our understanding of the controlling effect of these mental tools.

An Interesting Experiment

Ask someone to add up a column of figures quickly, saying the sum aloud as fast as you write them down, one number at a time. Starting with the number 1,000, followed by the numbers 20, 1,000, 30, 1,000, 40, and 1,000, the sum at that point is 4,090. If we are then asked to add the number 10, the answer received most often is 5,000, instead of the correct answer of 4,100.

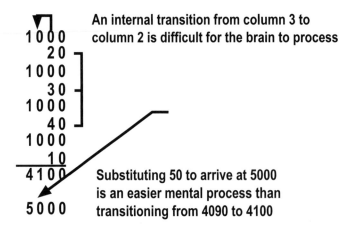

An internal transition from column 3 to column 2 is difficult for the brain to process

1 0 0 0
   2 0
1 0 0 0
   3 0
1 0 0 0
   4 0
1 0 0 0
   1 0
4 1 0 0

Substituting 50 to arrive at 5000 is an easier mental process than transitioning from 4090 to 4100

5 0 0 0

Try this on an audience, and intelligent people will actually argue with you, insisting that the real answer is 5,000. Try this on your bank teller. People will get upset that you differ with them. Yet this math problem is not associated with any emotion.

People answer the question incorrectly because a preparatory set was created in adding the figures. We have added 20, 30, and 40 in sequence and, therefore, have an unconscious expectation that the number 50 will be next. The *preparatory* set is the anticipation of the number 50.

When, instead, we are asked to add the number 10, we must transfer interior figures from the third to the second column. This is a difficult mental process because people normally process numerical information by bracketing numbers from the outside edges instead of thinking in terms of the middle. Instead of the more difficult mental process of an internal transfer, the mind easily substitutes the number 50 that we were expecting, incorrectly producing the number 5,000 for the sum of 4,090 and 10.

How Should My Beliefs Grow?

This simple math problem is a good example of the effect of preparatory set and how our own mind can deceive us, and yet this example is not based upon an emotion-laden belief. A person trained from early childhood with any particular belief will have value and emotions invested in his or her own belief. If asked to accept a contrary notion, people will respond emotionally. That is because the feeling that you experience at the moment of accepting a belief typically becomes associated with the belief from the time it is first acquired, and will be associated with that belief for the rest of your life. This is particularly true with those beliefs acquired at an early age before you had developed the ability to reason for yourself.

The emotions you experience with a belief when it is first accepted are forever a part of your belief. This is why our religious heritage has such a powerful effect on us. If you have been raised in a particular faith, you cannot simply ignore your own religious beliefs without suffering an adverse psychological effect except through non-threatening education. To leave childhood beliefs that were reinforced weekly behind as an adult requires significant education.

Because we naturally associate any belief with the emotions present when they originated, and because we cannot easily take any aspect of our lives out of its context, alternatives to our own scotomas are not only unacceptable, but can be threatening—even to the point where people are willing to risk their lives to defend their current notion of what they believe is right.

This phenomenon occurs today, when otherwise intelligent people become suicide bombers in the name of their religious beliefs. It has nothing to do with truth. A logical argument cannot defeat an emotional belief. Significant non-threatening education is required to cause behavioral change. In the Middle East today there is insufficient time for education. The result is that we are at war because of scotomas.

The mature way of accommodating childhood beliefs in the adult world and with reality is to continually redefine each concept, or belief, in order to keep it relevant. People cling to their own beliefs. However, even our religious beliefs should mature just like any other notion that influences our lives. A fear God concept is normal in childhood, but by adulthood a more abstract way of defining God is far more effective.

The myth of Santa Claus is accepted by children raised in the American Christian tradition. However, this only lasts for a few years because, eventually, Santa Claus is undermined by reality. Those who do not substitute the good of giving to others for their childish notion of Santa as "their gift giver" feel disappointed and suffer emotionally; whereas, those able to develop a healthy change of perception may continue to celebrate Santa with Christmas as their symbol of giving for the rest of their lives.

The objective in life is to continue to grow. If our beliefs evolve healthily, to the extent that we are able to live within our full range of needs through continued growth and development, we should eventually achieve a peak experience. Our goal should be for our individual life to continually become more fulfilled, richer, and more satisfying. Although the specific goals that fulfill our individual lives will be unique, understanding the universal process for human growth makes the journey easier.

This Life May Be Our Only Opportunity

Because humanists do not believe that life's reward is limited to achieving an immortal soul's existence, they feel that each individual must be responsible for living their own life fully in the present. Humanists feel that we should all make the most of each day while we are living on Earth—and certainly not sacrifice this life for a ticket to an afterlife that may not exist. If there is an afterlife, living a proper life should entitle everyone to whatever rewards are then available. In the meantime we should not miss living this life.

There may be a life after death, but we have no valid evidence it exists. If we believe in an afterlife we only have hope based upon blind faith to rely upon. Therefore, why would we want to sacrifice our lives on Earth with only the hope that a life in the hereafter exists, especially if it requires our denial of the opportunity to live our own life to the fullest here today?

Being a suicide bomber makes absolutely no intelligent sense. To a humanist, that person is sick. To deceive such a person, causing them to act against their own best interest of living his or her life on Earth to the fullest extent possible, with a promise of "vestal virgins in heaven," is ludicrous, and certainly a fraud on the individual believer, especially if there is no heaven hereafter.

Striving to maximize the opportunity to live on Earth can cause significant internal conflict. There are people in positions claiming authority that use control devices, such as insisting that heaven is restricted to only those who "believe" in their particular path.

Not only is that notion absurd, but why would anyone want to associate with a god that makes such unreasonable demands, particularly when it results in the vast majority of people in the world being denied immortality? That notion does a disservice to those who would otherwise live a quality life on Earth, and who instead feel that they must now spend their limited time on Earth in search of a ticket that each belief claims to have the only source. While it hardly makes sense, if that notion becomes a scotoma in childhood, intelligent people will be afraid to follow any other path.

Most humanists accept that those with this belief have every right to their own notion of truth—except for those who insist that it is their religious duty to see that others must follow the same prescription. Then it becomes offensive. Indeed, this thinking causes wars. Our society is still living on lower levels of Maslow's hierarchy; and we continue to have crusaders even today.

Many people experience trauma in struggling to move out of the cultural limitations of their own childhood. Many experience guilt, fear, or estrangement from society's mainstream. They may even experience it from their own parents, particularly when they challenge beliefs instilled in them by their parents.

Because any living person's, or institution's, first duty is to preserve itself, religions place many cultural barriers on growth to keep their adherents from escaping. Although most humanists consider themselves free of cultural religious barriers, each will still have some. Life is not simple. Ultimately, difficult as it was to get to this point of freedom from our cultural traditions, humanists find that focusing exclusively on this life, rather than being concerned with seeking an afterlife, is more exhilarating, and more than suffices. For humanists, our reason for existing is measured by how we live this life.

What Is God's Answer?

Human beings identify forces in nature that exceed our current ability to comprehend or understand. Such forces have historically been called a "god." Many primitive people felt that the Sun, or elements of the weather, or even the sea were gods. People prayed, or sacrificed to such god's for their own safety.

Prior to Abraham, many gods were acceptable. However, when religion required accepting only one god, the use of the term became more complex. As science explained away mysteries, which had once been associated with "gods," the definition of god became more abstract. We are still doing this today. "God" is a universal term used by most people for identifying whatever is beyond our own personal knowledge that we, as an individual, fear or revere.

We each have our own definition of God. There could be serious arguments in any congregation if all members were required to accept the same god concept. Many clergy explain "God" by expressing generalities, or adjectives that are universal, or are non-threatening because they describe the effects of God rather than defining what the term "God" actually means. That avoids conflict.

Claiming, for example, that "God is the Creator" says very little, but implies a lot. The concept of creator could be synonymous with God being nature. Obviously, if nature were your definition, the statement that "God is the Creator" would be true—assuming that the universe has not always existed. That notion, however, does not imply a caring god, or why do we have evil? Nor does this sort of god explain anything about our purpose, other than that we were created and are to live this life on Earth. Besides raising the question of whether there was intelligent thought behind our being here today, it has little utility.

Aristotle expanded the study of philosophy and introduced the notion that a central philosophic question is "why something occurs." Our religious views have evolved from that perspective. Humanism accepts that there may not be a reason "why" we have the opportunity to live. All that we know for sure is that our life exits. We are part of nature. There may not have been a beginning. Therefore, there may be no prime mover, or Creator.

Time is relevant to our existence, but if there are eleven dimensions, as theoretical physicists currently suggest as the result of quantum mechanics, our universe may have always existed in some form. Scientists accept that energy continually changes form, but they claim it has always existed.

Humanists do not ask "why." Instead we are content to only seek the answer of "how" things in our universe occur. Those questions are within the realm of science and, therefore our knowledge. They are testable to ascertain truth. Humanists see no reason to seek solutions beyond our current science. "Why?" may not be a valid question. There may not be an answer to a "why" question.

If one believes that there was an intelligent independent cause for life that we might call God, we might conclude there may be a divine purpose for our individual lives. However, if a person believes that Darwin was correct, all forms of life have evolved into more complex species through natural selection. There does not have to be a reason for our existence. Asking why we exist may be an invalid question.

Humanists accept that we humans are merely a part of the natural evolution of life, created by a natural evolutionary process of nature. That theory makes more logical sense than the notion that there was a prime mover. Who created the prime mover?

If we recognize that science is the closest that we can currently come to truth we could have different conclusions than many of our religious traditions. Some accept the hypothesis that God intentionally created us by design by accepting this notion "on faith." Others, however, recognize that facts, tested and proven by science, support a more obvious truth, and are more believable without requiring blind faith in an esoteric something that logic simply cannot support.

The statement that there is a "Creator God" ultimately expresses the postulate that powers exist in the universe that are superior to ourselves. That should be obvious. In reality people saying that "God is the Creator" may only be describing nature. Most people would not pray to nature. With a nature view of life we could still pray, or meditate, to tune our self to our own reality.

However, the notion of expecting a response from nature would not fulfill the needs of those who find prayer necessary for themselves. Their "God" must be more than the forces that created our universe for their comfort.

What About Those Who Claim To Be Atheists?

Except for those who are determined to deny someone else's beliefs, or are still fighting their own earlier god concept that has not matured, the term "god" does have utility for most people. That word denotes something very personal, and culturally it is used to express what we cannot discern, or that which we deeply revere or fear.

The more appropriate approach for those who do not believe that the god concept has value for themselves, and yet still feel compelled to challenge anyone else's right to use the term, should restrict their challenge to the more primitive definitions of the meaning of the term "God." Their objection is more appropriately addressed to those who require supernatural qualities in the definition of god. Some theologians today agree with Atheists who claim that Theism is no longer relevant, but these theologians all still accept Deism as valid.

Atheists gain little by denying another's right to use the term God in other contexts. For many people the term "God" has great emotional security value because they have no better way to express their concerns, or their awe of the unknown. There are powers in the universe that are greater than themselves. If that is their use of the term god, why object?

Churches exist on the social level. God is a security level belief for many people. Attacking anything on the social or security level sometimes results in violent response. All people will defend an attack on their social or security level. Non-threatening education is the best means of challenging beliefs on those levels. If the Atheist's goal is to reform another person's beliefs they should challenge supernatural definitions, not challenge a word that may validly have an actualized level definition.

Throughout the ages, wars have been caused because everyone "knows" that their own beliefs are true. Therefore, most fervently believe that everyone else's conflicting beliefs must be false. In reality there may be no truth regarding a faith belief. Truth may only exist "in the eye of the beholder."

Christians and Jews fight over whether Christ was the promised Messiah. Muslims and Christians fight over whether Mohammad was a later prophet sent by God. Muslims and Jews still fight over whose lineage represents the rightful descendants of Abraham. Who really are "God's chosen people?"

Yet there is dissension and discord even among major religious faiths. For example, even among those of the Islamic faith there is significant disagreement over relatively small details that lead people in the Mideast to kill each other to defend their own truth. The Iraq Constitution is a test of compromise over three radically differing views within the same religion. Evangelical Christians challenge all other Christians. Each has based their position on their view of historic facts that makes their interpretation the only valid truth, at least for themselves.

The Dead Sea Scrolls have proven to scholars that the "facts" upon which is based the "faith" currently accepted in our culture, may be false. Nevertheless, many continue to believe what they have always believed, and will defend their position to their death.

Why is that so? The answer may be seen in our previous discussion. Psychology has shown us how our minds work. Once we have a sufficient answer to our question, we may develop a scotoma that blocks any challenge. Our own truth becomes our own reality--but it is only true for ourselves, and even then should be only for that moment. Only through non-threatening education can we change that view.

Our Ultimate Concerns

Paul Tillich, widely recognized as the dean of Christian theologians, stated over sixty years ago that our personal definition of "God" describes our individual *"ultimate concern"*: the forces that drive our behavior, or the purpose toward which we direct our own life. For Tillich, "God" is not a person or a thing; "God" is our own personal belief in whatever empowers our life.

According to Tillich we each create our own God. Tillich claimed that since "God" is our own concept of what is ultimately important to each of us, God is whatever compels us to act, that which we must seek. With such a concept, "atheism" is absurd. Carried to an extreme, your own "God" could be money.

Tillich stated that we express our ultimate concerns in the form of symbols because we cannot fully describe our feelings in any other way. Our symbols become highly valued and form our own religious approach to life. Our "religious symbols" orient us toward our ultimate concerns.

Symbols are much like a painting. If you must describe the brush strokes and color you have missed the point. You look through a picture to see what it represents, to feel its subject.

We cannot deny our own religious symbols, especially those that were learned before the age of reason and are accompanied with emotions that we experienced in their formation, without risking negative psychological reactions, or even ultimately developing a neurosis. The best that we can safely do is for our symbols to grow with us to keep them relevant by continually redefining their meaning as we gain knowledge—or through education finding an alternate path to replace them with something we find better, or closer to the truth.

Our own symbols become a part of who we are from the day that they are accepted by us, including the emotions we experienced when they were accepted. These symbols must be redefined periodically if they are to remain meaningful, especially for a person whose knowledge of his or her universe has expanded beyond the symbols they represent. If this does not happen, our symbols will be abandoned, or rejected, as we mature. Since symbols are associated with the emotions present when they were adopted, outright rejecting them can be painful. Therefore, failing to redefine symbols to keep them relevant will put the person in unnecessary conflict with their own past.

As an example of a symbol, the meaning of a wedding ring cannot be adequately described in ten thousand words. The ring represents something far beyond a piece of metal. A wedding ring is not "truth," even though truth in the relationship is required to maintain a healthy marriage. When the ring becomes the thing that is valued instead of what it represents, it loses its real meaning.

Our own religious orientations are the symbols we use to express our own "ultimate concerns." If a symbol becomes valued beyond what it symbolizes or represents, it becomes an "icon." When we defend our symbols as "the truth," rather than what they represent to us, we then cease to communicate meaningfully to others, and have lost the real meaning of the symbol for our own self.

A Current View of Religion

Life is viewed through the lens you use. There is no view of life that is the only one that is valid. John Shelby Spong is a Bishop of the Episcopal Church today. Bishop Spong believes that Theism is dying and should be replaced with a Deistic, or more relevant view of God as the life force.

Bishop Spong states that Jesus was merely a human being who died just like all of us. It was later theologians that added the notion of Jesus resurrection. For Bishop Spong Jesus was a living Jew who had a very unique message. The story of Jesus was told by writers many years after his death. Because the life of Jesus was so profound for the Gospel writers they told their story in the context of the current Jewish Old Testament writing. Bishop Spong uniquely places the New Testament over the Old Testament and a different view of Jesus emerges.

According to Bishop Spong the purpose for Jesus's life was to teach us how to live our life here on Earth. Jesus's message was for us to live a good, moral and meaningful life to the highest level of actualization that we are capable of achieving while we are on Earth. For Bishop Spong Jesus was only concerned with life here on Earth. It was later Christianity that changed the message by adding myths that went beyond the life of the Jesus who actually lived on Earth. Followed to a logical conclusion, that makes Jesus into a humanist.

For people who have strong attachment to their early Christian symbols who claim to be humanists, that view can make their own religious experience far more meaningful.

Wouldn't it be interesting if all religious traditions eventually evolved to adopt the philosophy of humanism, even though their view may be expressed with their historic symbols? It would be one way for organized religions to continue to exist by always remaining relevant as truth unfolds. Judaism has the *Society of Humanistic Judaism*, the American Humanist Association has the *Humanist Society* to address those needs within humanism.

Maslow's Gods

Maslow found that an individual's "God" concepts varied depending upon the need level upon which they are then religiously living. A "fear God" concept may be the only way someone living predominantly on the basic, or security level, can perceive his or her "God" as a force. On the social level, a "father God" concept may be more acceptable. "God" may be a synonymous term for nature on the actualized level.

Some people living on higher need levels use terms like "love," "freedom," "spirituality," or "life force" when defining their "God." This expresses forces they deem important or paramount to their own existence. It may be easy for some to use the term "God" to express their reverence for life. Life, obviously, is something that we do not fully comprehend.

Many humanists use the term only to communicate with others who have a lower need level concept. Most humanists are more apt to express an awe of their natural world, using terms expressing their reverence for life.

For a person who has an "actualized God" concept, like a person who uses "God" as a synonym for nature, it would be ridiculous to deny God's existence by claiming to be an atheist. For these people the term "atheist" is repugnant. That term is not only anti-social for its negative effect on others, but it is also irrelevant. How can anyone deny the existence of nature? Most humanists accept that there is no value in denying anyone else's deeply felt belief.

Humanism is not atheistic, although most atheists may also be humanists. Humanism, as a philosophy of life, could possibly be categorized as agnostic because the use of the term "God" is not relevant to humanism. All humans should recognize that some forces of nature in the universe are superior to their own existence—whatever term they use to describe them is up to them. Atheists simply cannot accept using the term "God" in any form.

Atheism expresses only that the proponent is opposed to the use of the term "God" for any purpose. However, that stance does not say what the individual expressing it actually stands for. We know what they do not believe. The more important question is, what do they believe? Filling that need is why many atheists identify with humanism. Humanism is a positive philosophy of life without any requirement of accepting truths based solely upon faith, or the necessity of adopting any religion, in order for a person to have a full, ethical, and successful life here on Earth. Some people identify themselves as humanists, but also subscribe to a personal belief or religion that goes beyond the humanist philosophy for social or cultural reasons, such as family tradition.

Humanists seldom attack another person's beliefs because humanism advocates personal freedom for everyone to embrace life to its fullest as they so choose. The best that humanists can offer is affirmative education that allows a person's religious views to more realistically mature in a positive effort to help people understand the value of fully living their life on Earth today.

Where all humanists may validly object is when "supernatural" requirements are necessary as a prerequisite to use the term "God." All humanists object to a "supernatural" characteristic for God because at that point there is no discernable test for reality, truth or veracity, but only subjective belief, or blind faith.

Humanists find no valid reason to base our lives merely on blind faith. That would risk reducing the measure of truth to the level of absurdity. We may not fully understand nature now, but that does not mean humans never will. A supernatural belief becomes unnecessary. Humanists do not feel that they have to have an answer for every question to be able to live a good life.

There are many additional aspects of understanding the subject of God that go beyond the parameters of this discussion. We know for a fact that we are currently unable to fully comprehend nature. The important point here is that our approach for understanding those forces beyond ourselves is currently deeply personal. No one so far has discovered the "truth," and the use of the term "God" has no clear definition.

Because of a lack of education, or exposure to different opinions, some feel compelled to answer certain of their questions of life with myth or lore. Challenging their faith would leave them without an alternative belief system. Therefore, real harm, and little value, is found in an unsolicited challenges of another's deeply felt beliefs.

The result of gratuitously attacking another's deeply felt beliefs may cause irreparable harm, not only to the believer, but also to the attacker. Such behavior generally will not make anyone feel better, so why do it? Most humanists are capable of recognizing the effect such behavior would have upon others and would not intentionally do so. An ethical humanist normally does not intentionally harm others.

Maslow acknowledged that all humans are subject to cultural and psychological restraints. Once a notion is acceptable to a person, it can easily be developed into a limiting scotoma. We can become blind to the effect of our negative behavior just like we block any information challenging a deeply felt belief.

Try telling those who are still fighting their parents' God concept that atheism is irrelevant. Their view of the God concept is limited to a narrow range, and because of this barrier, they must expend energy defending their position because they are fighting the "God" concept of their childhood. They may even feel justified offending others' beliefs in their zeal. Their God concept simply did not mature as they grew, forcing them to now waste their limited energy, much like Don Quixote, did fighting windmills.

Many atheists are unaware that what they are objecting to is their own limited definition of "God," and not the legitimate practice of calling whatever forces are beyond us "God." They are validly objecting to the notion of supernaturalism, which they assume is necessary for the use of the term God. However, they fail to make the distinction. Because they find no utility in the use of the word, their belief is that the word simply should not be used. Most people disagree. A more constructive approach would be to challenge their definition.

Most humanists do not worry about such concerns. When I asked Stephen Hawking's colleague as a theoretical physicist, Steven Weinberg, a humanist Nobel Laureate in physics, about his view of God, he responded, "Why would I even worry about such things?" Such effort is trivial and of little value for many humanists.

Most atheists can accept humanism as a valid life view, but many humanists do not accept atheism as adding relevance to life. Why offend others with a negative belief when humanism has so many positive arguments to make that support life? Education is the only valid socially acceptable approach for changing others opinions. Negatively challenging another's belief system is not acceptable. Most humanists simply do not worry about the subject.

God and Spirituality

According to Harvard's distinguished humanist professor, Edward O. Wilson, the founder of sociobiology, everyone has some *spiritual need*; that is, a biological need to connect with nature.

Sociobiology is the study linking the field of biology with sociology. According to Wilson, biology does not end at birth with the study of everything that occurs in our lives thereafter exclusively in the field of sociology. Wilson finds that many of our institutions, including the human need for spirituality, are biologically determined.

All healthy people have a natural spiritual awe of our universe. People may label their reverence for life however they wish.

Spiritualism is a human characteristic. It is not the exclusive province of religion. How it is recognized are issues everyone is biologically compelled to reconcile for him or herself.

Realizing that it does little good to challenge another's beliefs, humanists can accept that each person is entitled to live his or her own life as they choose—at least until they attempt to limit the rights, or to challenge the beliefs, of others. The religious far right and the atheist far left are both in the wrong when they use an "in your face" approach to proselytize their "faith."

The only valid way to change another's belief is to provide a non-threatening opportunity for the introduction of empirically based new evidence so that a person's view of life may grow through education. Only non-threatening education can change a person's view of their own truth. To be effective, people have to be receptive to another view. Our attitude must be open and receptive for new ideas to take root. New ideas can only ultimately be accepted if they are properly presented in a non-threatening manner.

So What Has God Told Us?

So what have we learned about why are we here from God? The truth is that we have not learned anything that is empirically testable. People only choose to believe what they are willing to accept to be true. Those who are not humanists may even then claim the answer came from their god.

For most people their own notion is acceptable, and that is all that matters. Many people are content within their own scotomas. However, those who must have testable proof, or reason, and, therefore, cannot accept answers based upon blind faith, are left without an answer. It does little good to attack the God concept for not providing an answer.

Nevertheless, the use of the term "God" still has validity for many people today. There does not have to be a supernatural element for the term "God" to have relevance for some, or simply to provide utility in communicating with others.

Each person can live an equally good life on Earth, fulfilling whatever is important for him or herself, without having to unnecessarily cause conflict with those of different worldviews or opinions. The members of any congregation will be unable to agree upon a single definition of God, unless they blindly follow their leader. But we will only have a stable society if we each are willing to allow others the right to have their own view of life. All we can truthfully say is that God has not answered the question of why we are here on Earth for everyone.

How Do We Face Our Own Death?

We are capable of accepting that we are here to experience our own journey through this life. By the time our journey is completed, the life of each of us will have hopefully been fulfilled. Maslow concluded that when people reach the point of complete actualization, they arrive at a state of mind where even their own death is non-threatening.

For most people elementary school was a great experience during the earliest part of life, preparing us for the next level of our growth. Few feel the need to repeat the experience, although we may still enjoy seeing the benefit of the early school experience in the lives of our children and grandchildren. Though it is a good experience for young children, most people are relieved that elementary school is no longer important for them in their later years. For that part of our life we adults are now fulfilled. We do not want to go back and start over.

Similarly, if we have actualized our own life, having experienced life to its fullest, we will no longer need to fear death. We can then recognize that death is inevitable—while it is not sought after, it is also no longer an object of concern. When we need to experience nothing further for our own life to be fulfilled, death can be accepted as a natural conclusion of our life.

As our bodies deteriorate our own death may legitimately be sought. Having reached his elder years, and having fully experienced life, Corliss Lamont, (widely considered the "dean" of humanism in the early years of the American Humanist Association) demonstrated death with dignity, peacefully sitting in his backyard facing the sun, and quietly passed away. From this perspective, death is as natural as living, and the notion of life after death is not necessary in order for our lives to be fulfilled. When we no longer spend our life fearing death, maximizing our own existence while we are living on Earth, protecting our family and preserving our life's work will be far more relevant and rewarding.

Why Do We Need Others?

Humans are not self-sufficient. From birth we are dependent upon others. Growing into a fully functioning, healthy person without support from others is impossible. Knowing that we need others for us to even exist, the issue is: *what is the ideal relationship that we should seek with others?*

Martin Buber, a noted Jewish theologian and philosopher, recognized what we gain by accepting another person for whom they are, without judgment, or attempting to influence them. This relationship is necessary if we are to acquire another's true perspective to aid us in our struggle to achieve our full potential. The benefit that results from a healthy relationship—harmonizing with another person without trying to change him or her—is enormous. Buber identified this relationship as the *"I-Thou."*

We know the depth perspective we experience driving down a highway using both eyes, in contrast with driving while closing one eye. Much like the advantage of perceiving three dimensions by using two eyes, complete understanding and acceptance of another person gives us perspective for understanding ourselves. A healthy self-image is derived only through being accepted, and being fully understood, by another person. The feelings achieved from belonging to a community, or being held in high regard by others, are important for our own growth. Therefore, healthy relationships with others become very important, and are necessary for our own life to become significant.

Without healthy relationships with others our self-image becomes protective and is, in itself, a barrier to achieving fulfillment. We only grow as a healthy person through our relationships with others. The better our relationships with others, the healthier we can become. Thus, like digging in the sand, where the more we dig the more sand falls back in the hole, the more in depth relationships with others we experience, the more we grow.

An Episcopal priest once proved to me that we are unable to give enough of ourselves to others. He has spent his entire life giving his all, caring for his parishioners and everyone else that he encountered, without worrying about any of his own needs. Yet he never went without, even though he could not have anticipated the source of his needs satisfaction. In fact, he has lived an abundant life. The more we offer of ourselves to others, the more comes back to us in unpredictable ways. Everyone benefits. Life is far more exciting when we do everything that we can to caringly, and unselfishly, give of ourselves for the benefit of others.

People need close relationships with others throughout life to become truly fulfilled. The recognition of inter-need dependence for need satisfaction, which exists between two or more people, is what we identify as "love." The character of love, like all other orientations to life, changes as individuals exist on different need levels. The basic level produces stronger emotions, with survival and sex producing the strongest drives. On the social level, the warmth of sharing is evident. On the actualized level, love may be found between soul-mates, whose lives are truly integrated together. To be most effective, love must be shared in an "*I-thou*" relationship.

Our Differing Purposes

Although, according to Maslow, all people have the same hierarchical need structure, even though each individual approaches satisfying their needs differently. Just how different humans are can best be understood by contrasting our psychological temperament types. Since the time of Aristotle, it has been known that people have primarily four distinctly different types of personality temperaments. Each type thinks and approaches life from distinctly different points of view.

Hypocrites outlined this theory in 370 B.C. There are those of us who live within cultural parameters, providing for others, and those living creatively outside of our societal norms. There are those who comprehend their world, and seek lofty goals, and there are those searching for each step to get a foothold necessary to get there.

Each personality type consists of standards, or values, which adherents share with everyone else in the same temperament type. It would be rare, if not impossible, for an individual to fit completely into more than one of these basic psychological types, although most people do display some secondary characteristics of another type. However, the secondary characteristic serves only as a modifier of each person's primary style of thinking.

Although, with effort, all people are capable of behavior outside the limitations of their specific temperament style, it is quite difficult, and usually must be specifically learned; much like learning to write your name with the opposite hand. It will not be natural. We each remain our same temperament type for our entire lifetime.

In the early 1950's Isabel Meyers, and her mother, Kathryn Briggs, brought substance to the ancient psychological temperament type theory by devising a simple questionnaire for identifying type. David Keirsey—who authored an excellent book called *Please Understand Me II*—sets forth a simple test to ascertain our personal temperament type. His more recent work amplified Meyers-Briggs' explanation of temperament type theory. After describing each personality type in detail, Keirsey then shows how differing types interact. You feel like Keirsey knows you personally. In a few pages of reading you not only know yourself, but can also understand your potential areas of conflict with your life partner or co-workers.

Psychologists make the point that we are only able to maximize our lives on Earth, and become fully actualized, if we follow a path consistent with our own personality type. Requiring behavior inconsistent with your own type can cause neurosis.

We cannot walk in someone else's shoes; we must create our own path. But in order to do that, we must first understand ourselves. It is very beneficial, in actualizing ourselves through our relationships with others, to know which personality type we have, and what that means for us. It is even more effective when we can also understand the personality type of those with whom we closely relate.

I have identified my own type, as defined by Meyers-Briggs, as an *idealist*. This is a rare type, found in less than ten percent of society. According to Keirsey, I am further identified as an *idealist-idealist*, which he calls a *"counselor"* because I have no other secondary characteristic. That type is very rare. Less than one percent of our society view information by processing it in the same manner that I am compelled to do. Understanding the sixteen differing types described by Keirsey is a significant benefit in understanding others.

Idealists are unable to see themselves. We require recognition from others to find self-worth—and constantly must seek validation, so we are compelled to spend our lives giving to others. Though idealists are capable of solving other people's problems relatively naturally, idealists generally cannot solve their own problems without help from others. Although idealists are incapable of seeing themselves, idealists easily see the big picture for others and are able to instantly put complex issues in proper perspective for them. But don't bother an idealist with details. Because they must quickly find a solution, idealists become frustrated when a person must explain a situation by relating each and every detail.

My wife is the exact opposite of me; she is a *rationalist*. They are even rarer, representing only six percent of society. For rationalists, who are able to validate themselves from within, imposing the requirement to serve others is seriously frustrating. Rationalists will serve others, but only by choice. They do not feel the compelling need to do so.

My wife must understand each step in any process for herself first before she can proceed to the next step. In contrast, I leap to conclusions. I would find her thought process frustrating, but for her it is essential. Truth is her most important consideration. She can only discover truth by observing every fact. My wife finds the journey more important, and rewarding, than the objective. She gets so absorbed in what she is seeing on her journey that she may forget where she was going. My mind is already there, but I cannot remember the route that I traveled.

We discovered our differences the first time we bought a birthday card for a friend. I immediately found a card containing an appropriate message for the friend, with an acceptable design. I was ready to buy the card and get on with life. My wife, however, was unwilling to buy any card until she examined every one, to make sure the one we chose was the very best available. We proceeded to frustrate each other, due solely because of our differing personality types. If we had not discovered the Meyers-Briggs theory, our relationship undoubtedly could not have survived. This is serious stuff.

We now have agreed to compromise. If I find a card that I like, I am free to proceed to the register. In the meantime, my wife continues to examine all other cards. If she finds a better card before I have paid, I will purchase her card instead, without question. If I have already paid for my card, my wife has agreed to leave with me, now feeling that she has at least done her best. We recognize that this solution may not be perfect, but it works for us.

On the other hand, we have also enlarged our own experiences by observing the world through each other's eyes. When we take time to appreciate nature, I am more interested in how what we are seeing integrates into the natural world. My wife sees a bunny in the road, stops to smell the flowers beside our path, and gets totally immersed in the setting, while I am more apt to seek the end of the path, wondering where it leads. We have discovered that neither of us is "wrong," but that we are simply different.

Shakespeare puts it well: "*Nothing is either 'right nor wrong,' but thinking makes it so.*" Life is much richer when it can be appreciated from another's perspective. To be effective, however, this must be achieved through an *I-thou* relationship, without attempting to change the other person.

A different perspective is that of *guardians*. They make up the largest number of personality types, which Meyers-Briggs found in approximately forty-five percent of society. Guardians expect everyone to abide by "the rules", and they expend significant effort assuring that they do. Guardians make wonderful schoolteachers, police officers, homemakers, ministers, nurses, and physicians—occupations in which dependability and their need to provide for others are their primary concerns. They get things done instantly, without question, because they feel obligated, since it is the "right thing to do." In turn, they also make sure that everyone else is doing their job. Guardians need constant praise for their services, however, or they will resent having to serve.

The rest of society may be classified as *artisans*. People with this personality type are capable of seeing the world without restraint. They do not like routine, and may ignore social norms, because they cannot accept living "inside of the box."Artisans obviously make great artists, but they are also frequently good musicians, actors, advertising agents, or politicians. Many artisans, however, are also incorrigible criminals and social deviants. Artisans can really frustrate guardians, who feel that no one should ignore the rules. By contrast, a rationalist can ignore an artisan unless imposed upon. An idealist can appreciate the creativity of an artisan, but will have little tolerance for any deviation that does not move toward a positive goal.

If a church dinner is being organized, for example, guardians are the ones who manage it—but do not misspell their name in the church bulletin! If the church fails to provide recognition, the rationalist may not notice, and the idealist would stop participating. The guardian would resent it, but would begrudgingly continue to serve out of a sense of duty. In the meantime, guardians would be infuriated with the idealist for quitting. The rationalist would still be washing the dishes, ignoring everyone else—doing their job just because it needs to be done. The artisans may not show up to prepare for the dinner at all— and if they did, they would be decorating the tables.

So, what does all this have to do with the quality of our life? Everything! Success can only be measured personally. Increasing our self-awareness will in turn increase our opportunity for living a successful life. Not knowing who we are leaves us vulnerable. Assuming others think from our perspective, or personality type, could be disastrous for any relationship. Thus, first knowing ourselves becomes essential for our own happiness. Understanding and appreciating the differences in others improves the quality of our own life.

When a companion stops to examine the flowers, for example, idealists can react in one of two ways: they can become irritated and impatient to get where they are going, or they can see an opportunity to expand their own horizon. One approach limits their existence;

the other enhances their life. Understanding the differences between ourselves and another can only expand our experience, and enrich life far beyond what each of us could achieve individually.

The rationalist asks the idealist, artisan, or guardian to "stop and smell the roses." The idealist expands the other types' horizons and goals. The guardian can feel more genuine with the idealist, inspired by the artisan, and more genuinely understood by the rationalist while they diligently serve others. The artisan may create works of art and beauty for all to enjoy and not care that they act differently than anyone else. Interaction with each type will provide a different result. Combining personality types in a relationship enhances both, but only if each can accept the other as they are in an *I-thou* relationship.

Keirsey, in amplifying upon the Meyers-Briggs theory, found that, although we each have only one primary type, most of us have a predominant secondary characteristic, incorporating one of the other types, that modifies our behavior, but to a much lesser extent than our primary type. Thus, people may be best understood by recognizing in which of the sixteen categories they live.

By understanding psychological types we can reduce the chance of a weakness in our own psychological type becoming a dominant weakness and causing barriers in our relationships with others. By understanding each category we can be even more effective in maximizing the quality of our life. Others can help us create new paths around our barriers better than we could ever accomplish on our own. We created, or accepted, a barrier for some reason. It takes others providing new information for us to be able bridge or circumvent our own barriers.

By fully utilizing our individual strengths, and bridging our weaknesses with the strengths of others, we can enhance both our own existence, and our relationships with others. The effect is like a spiral. We are better able to fulfill our own life when we share our journey with others. As we share, we grow. As we grow we are better able to actualize our own existence, and to help others maximize theirs—but only if we are willing to allow others to be their genuine self. Thus a successful life is a spiral that continually grows through our relationship with others.

Why Should We Make Our Lives Significant?

After years of contemplation, I have found that, ultimately, only two aspects of life hold relevance for me. First, *our own life is meaningful to the extent we share in happiness*. By achieving actualization in the manner articulated by Maslow, we can reach the pinnacle of our own existence. However, that alone can cause one to become selfish and to miss the greater values in life that come from sharing our existence with others. Therefore, the second relevant element is equally necessary.

Simply stated, *our lives become significant to the extent the world becomes a better place because we have lived*. Thus, we are responsible for not only actualizing our own existence, but also for assisting others to achieve the highest quality of life they can attain, both now and in the future. Acting together we can achieve far more than anyone could accomplish individually. The healthy person keeps both of these values in balance.

This philosophic approach to life is consistent with Maslow's hierarchy of needs. Living one's life to the fullest by actualizing our existence makes our life meaningful. Extending our own existence by transcending ourselves in order that we may make a contribution to the lives of others, helps make our own life significant for ourselves, as well as adding value to the lives of others.

Many other contributions can be made by collectively working to improve our world. Our own life effort should be to add value. By focusing our attention on constructive issues, and providing solutions, we raise our awareness of opportunities to serve. We hopefully motivate ourselves to action in the process, and we also influence others to act whenever such an opportunity is presented to them.

How Do We Apply All of This?

I know a mentally challenged person whose life is dependent upon Good Will Industries. If they did not exist, my friend could be among the homeless and wandering the streets upon the loss of his support network; or he would not survive. By himself, he could not exist above Maslow's basic level of existence. Even now, with the continual assistance of others, he barely lives on the lower social level–although, this is at least two need levels above what he could accomplish by himself. Does this make his life insignificant, or not worth living? Not to him.

For my friend, his own existence may be all that is relevant—and yet he still cares about others. He feels that he is doing a good deed by smiling and saying "hello" to everyone he meets. He knows no strangers. He does not need to write a book or play a piano to make his own life meaningful. As a matter of fact, it may be easier for my friend to actualize his own existence than for anyone else I know; because, although he has some intellectual barriers to overcome, he does not create many psychological barriers for himself. We more "normal" folk have far more barriers, because we absorb cultural limitations, and establish artificial goals that my friend does not perceive.

Moreover, because my friend is so good-hearted, those who care for him—no matter what personality type—are able to recognize that they enhance their own lives by helping him. The guardian's effort to enrich my friend's life gives him or her a sense of purpose. The idealist gains satisfaction from serving on the Good Will board or fundraising for the organization. The rationalist finds value in buying products sold at the Good Will store. An artisan probably designed the brochure that helped raise money for the institution.

The real purpose for each person's participation is not only to serve my friend; it is for each person to fulfill his or her own needs or purpose through that effort. Everyone continually struggles to improve their current position in life, socially and economically, and to enhance their own sense of self-worth. No action is entirely altruistic. We are motivated to help my friend in order to gain fulfillment for ourselves, each in our own way. As a side benefit, we all know that we are doing something worthwhile for a good person who needs our help.

What Can We Do Collectively?

One purpose of formal education should be to reduce cultural barriers that inhibit normal growth and actualization—if not for the public at large (who are frequently bound with scotomas on any subject we are trying to communicate), at least for the more informed people who more easily recognize such barriers. The masses are typically ignorant on any given subject.

Provided the opportunity without physical, cultural, and self-imposed barriers people will actualize at their own rate, and in their own manner, based upon their own unique personality, educational opportunities, and needs. We cannot change all of society. But the opportunity must be available, and cultural and environmental obstacles to growth must be identified and eliminated, for anyone to be able to live on the highest levels. All of us do not have to actualize our own life for our society to be successful, but a successful society must allow each person to have the opportunity to do so.

Our constitutional form of government, as proclaimed in the Declaration of Independence, claims that we have "the right" to *life, liberty and the pursuit of happiness*, but it does not require our government to give us the means for achieving it. Our government only allows each of us the right. We are not guaranteed success. We must earn that for ourselves.

One cultural barrier, for example, is the lack of public awareness of the different personality types, and the implications that has for understanding each other. As previously stated, understanding our differences in thinking and motivation can improve everyone's quality of life by reducing miscommunication. Accepting the diversity in other people has great personal value. The differences between us helps each of us grow.

Another barrier is most people's limited ability to relate to those living on other psychological levels of need. Even governments operate on differing need levels on Maslow's scale. It is unrealistic, for example, to expect the Russian public at large, generally existing on the high security/low social level, to appreciate the cultural concerns of Americans, who generally exist on a high social/low ego level. Nor can the typical Afghan Muslim be expected to appreciate our way of life.

People must first be taught to recognize these differing levels, and then how to speak more effectively to those with whom we wish to communicate, by first communicating on their level of living. Similar to Maslow's problem of understanding a joke, or appreciating music, communication must begin on the lowest need level of those communicating. Teaching the public to identify and understand others' need levels could make a significant difference in meaningful communication.

Another barrier is caused by our educational methods. This can be effectively challenged without threatening anyone's belief system. Frank Goble, author of *The Third Force*, a book amplifying Maslow's humanistic psychology, proposes an educational philosophy offering optimizing human awareness, helping all people to create, grow, and control their own choices and goals.

Goble contends that understanding humanistic psychology can help provide early educational opportunities tailored to each child's needs, rather than using pre-established educational patterns that may be inconsistent with individual needs. By designing our educational strategies to approach each individual within their own temperament type, we will enhance their learning. Making everyone fit into the same box does not effectively work to maximize growth. This change in how we approach education could dramatically enhance the opportunity for children to fully actualize their existence.

How Do I Make A Difference In My Own Life?

The message for each of us is to fully become ourselves—but first we must know ourselves. Only then can we become authentic and achieve a meaningful fulfillment of our own life. Maslow contributed by providing a means for understanding the process by which each of us can become fulfilled. We must provide the goals, or path, for ourselves. The way we apply our lives to make the world better and provide meaning to our personal lives will be unique to each of us. We each need to start toward our own actualization by defining our own mission in life. Otherwise daily living will define us, and because of cultural limitations we may miss the opportunity to fulfill ourselves.

Happiness is the feeling of contentment we experience while following the path toward total fulfillment. At the moment of a peak experience we will have an exhilarating, and possibly scary, feeling of total awareness—we will gain a rare insight into our personal universe. At those moments, we will know that we are then totally fulfilled, and have actualized our own life. Sharing our lives with others enhances our opportunities. We can now understand that the differences in each of us are what make life challenging and exciting. The world would be a dull place if we were all alike.

As I previously stated, as an idealist, only two aspects of life are relevant for me. *My life is meaningful to the extent I am able to achieve actualization. My life will be significant to the extent that the world is a better place because I have been here.* To be healthy, I must keep both in balance.

Considering only these two values, of the many leading to a successful life, others will respond very differently to the same circumstances. The response to additional values will be equally different; thus, there are multiple approaches to a successful life. To illustrate the point:

> If you are an artisan, you might say: "My life is meaningful to the extent that I am creatively engaged, and to the degree that I am excited about life's opportunities. My life is significant when I have made a uniquely creative work that is really mine, and is genuinely prized by others."

> A guardian may say: "My life is meaningful when I am accepted by others I care about; when I know that my family and loved ones are safe, and when my world feels in order. My life is significant when I am in charge of what I do, and I am appreciated by others for what I provide."

> A rationalist could say: "My life is meaningful when it is peaceful, when I know what is true, and I am fully functioning in the world— at least to the degree that I am then comfortable in my role. My life is significant when I feel my own contribution has succeeded better than my previous efforts, and when I know that my efforts are right."

These statements may be valid only momentarily, and will typically vary as we mature and as our mission in life becomes continually more focused. The younger rationalist, for example, may be more concerned with understanding how he or she is to accomplish a specific task. Upon aging, however, the need to know grows, and he or she eventually may want to know how *everything* works. Goals for all other personality types similarly change. Nothing human is etched in stone; nor should it be, including our own religious views.

Although everyone's approach to life is "hard wired," what an individual finds important at any given moment will only be tentative. The method by which we process information remains consistent through our lifetime. However, our individual method of processing information is similar only to others with the same psychological temperament type and how we implement our actions may differ from others of the same type because of our level of growth, maturation, and level of education. Thus, we will all appear different, even though those of the same temperament type will always process information in the same way.

Fortunately, there is no universal truth and no single answer to life's purpose—however, most of us will continue to assume everyone else understands us and should agree with us and, therefore, must think like we do. Fortunately they do not. Imagine how boring the world would be if everyone had to agree. Our personal mission statement is only valid for ourselves, but even that may change. There are very few absolute truths that we can all accept. The fact that each person will approach their actualization in a different way is good for society, because these differences enhance the quality of all of our lives by expanding our vision.

In Conclusion

What all of this means is that—even recognizing that we ultimately will physically become space dust—our existence still has meaning. Should we say that the Sun has no current value because its light will eventually become extinguished even though it was formed and has existed for millions of years? The Suns value is in providing sustenance, contributing to the panoply of life, and offering all of us a chance to live. It gives us the opportunity for happiness and meaning in our lives. It does not have to exist forever to have value.

The truth is that we know very little about anything. We know even less about how and why our own life came to be. We can only act upon what we know, or what we are willing to believe. Even though humans might not be immortal, our individual lives are valuable to ourselves today. To exist for any interval of time requires us to contribute as if there will always be a future. Life is sufficient justification for itself. Nothing else is necessary for our own life to have meaning. Whatever else we may choose to believe can only add to the meaning of our own life, but only for ourselves.

Instead of feeling that they are giving up something valuable, those who accept the notion that this life could possibly be all that there is express a sense of appreciation for the opportunity to maximize their own existence while here on Earth today. The freedom that comes from not having to seek an afterlife encourages those not seeking an afterlife to maximize their own opportunities here on Earth because there are no longer inhibiting barriers. At least they do not lose the opportunity to fully live the only life we know. To the contrary, people with this view find that they must put even more effort into their life on Earth. Because this may be all that there is, they feel a greater need to achieve actualization, thus fulfilling their own life's purpose.

All that anyone really can verify is that we live our own life today for ourselves and those we love. Anything more is essentially a matter of faith, and not fact. However, even those who choose to believe there must be an afterlife benefit by fulfilling their own existence while here on Earth.

We may be here through a fluke of nature, but we do exist. Humans are part of the natural evolution of life. It is not really possible to know whether individuals exist only to foster the evolution of the human species or whether there may be a deeper, more specific purpose for each of us as individuals. We can only believe that we know. All that we really do know for certain is that, as individuals, we only have one opportunity to live. Our immediate objective is to live our own life here today, striving to be the very best that we can become.

By showing us that higher levels of living exist, Maslow has helped us understand how to enrich our own lives by providing a path to actualize our existence. By limiting barriers, and fulfilling all of our needs on all levels of living, we are able to grow and expand our own life.

We know now that we must discover the specific path for ourselves. When we achieve a peak experience, we will then know we have fulfilled our own life, at least for that moment. When we have done our best to assist others in their journey, our lives will have significance. By fulfilling our own mission statement—e.g., "our lives are meaningful to ourselves and significant to others"—our own life will have then served its purpose.

At some point, death is inevitable. For those who believe that the soul and body separate after death, actualizing their existence while here on Earth should only enhance this opportunity. By actualizing their existence, their life will not have been wasted by missing an opportunity to live primarily for the hereafter. This approach to life should not conflict with any intelligent religious view. If it does, an educated person should question the value of such a limiting view. Those with faith may win even more by actualizing their existence here on Earth—particularly if they are correct.

Today many people are content believing that this life is all that exists. No one knows for certain. Hopefully for all of us—by actualizing our own existence—and thus knowing that we have lived a full life while we are here, we will be able to peacefully accept the end of our own life when the time comes. We should need nothing else for our own life to have had purpose and meaning.

To leave the world better than we found it, even humanists can agree, is an acceptable form of immortality. Like our Sun, or a flower in the forest, when we have lived this life to its fullest, there need be nothing further for our own life to be important.

For us, at least, our own life will then have had purpose. If we can then go out making the winning run by sliding safely into home plate shouting, "**Wow! What a trip!**" we will know that our own life has been fulfilled.

Addendum
A DECLARATION OF HUMANISM
A Humanist Ethic

Addendum
A DECLARATION OF HUMANISM
A Humanist Ethic

I.

Humanism is a philosophy, or an approach for living life on Earth. It starts with the premise that we are part of nature and only know for certain that we are living this life today. Certain aspects of life have value for living a good life. Consistent with this philosophy, I personally believe that a healthy person grows through the following stages, normally in this order.

This is my philosophic and ethical approach for living my life:

1. Existence. My body is my temple of life, and health is essential for my existence. This life is all that I can say I possess for certain.

2. Responsibility. I must assume the sole responsibility for my life. My behavior is within my control. I can only make my choices as I allow myself to live in the present. My personal attitude is within my control. A positive attitude enhances my chances for success.

3. Meaning. My life is meaningful to me to the extent my own needs are satisfied, and I achieve the homeostatic state of happiness. There need not be a universal purpose for my life to have meaning. My own life is sufficient purpose for living.

4. Security. To secure my opportunities, I must support justice for all, and respect the freedom of choice of everyone else for me to have the opportunity for justice. Justice is a progressive attainment of equality, limited only by the unique constraints of each person. Force should be tolerated only to suppress force that would otherwise inflict a person's unwarranted will over another person.

5. Social Relations. Human interdependence is essential for health and growth. I must be willing to give mutual respect and trust to maintain close personal relationships. I can recognize the relationship of inter-need dependence with others as love. I allow those I love within my defense mechanisms so that we might share our lives together for our mutual support. I must allow all others to be themselves. I strive to maintain I-Thou relationships with others.

6. <u>Actualization of Life.</u> My purpose for living is to experience the joy of life, and to actualize my growth to my fullest potential as a human being, consistent with my responsibility to others, and within the personal, environmental, and social resources available to me. I have an awe and spiritual reverence for nature while living my life as a part of the natural universe, and recognize that I am a steward of its resources each day while I am on Earth. I do not live my life on Earth with any expectations of a life after death.

7. <u>Commitment to Others.</u> My life becomes significant to the extent I assist others to actualize their own lives. I believe that achieving the highest quality of life as a healthy, mature person means balancing the meaningfulness of my life with my significance to others. Only in consort and harmony with others will my own life reach its maximum potential.

8. <u>Knowledge.</u> I feel that it is essential to maintain the conditions of free inquiry and an open society in order to encourage the expression of all ideas. The expansion of knowledge can ultimately result in the best choices for the growth of everyone. I support using all means available for ascertaining the truth, and applying the results obtained to improve the welfare of all life on Earth. My values and standards are relative and malleable as new experiences and information shapes my worldview.

9. <u>Social Institutions.</u> Within my own resources, I encourage people I encounter, as well as governments and other institutions, to reduce and eliminate all barriers to personal growth, and to provide optimum conditions for the healthy development of all people. The democratic process assures the greatest opportunity for most people. We live in a world economy. World government should assure peace from physical conflict for all people on Earth.

10. <u>Interdependence of Life.</u> I affirm the wonder and beauty of nature as the creative process from which we humans have evolved; and I thereby recognize the unity and interdependence of, and feel respect for, all life on Earth. All people must share responsibility for the maintenance of the natural order of our planet. Life is sacred. However, over population of any species may threaten the opportunity for a quality life for all species. Humans are not an exception. Nature attempts to maintain a healthy balance. All living creatures on Earth must share our world together in harmony and balance if we are to survive and grow to our full potential.

II.

Additional expressions, such as an emotional attachment to a particular religious view, are very personal. They arise from previous experiences that have oriented our individual lives. We are each entitled to have our own. Therefore, our religious views of life should not be imposed upon others.

Lyle L. Simpson

Humanist Manifesto III

Thirty-four people, primarily Unitarian ministers and philosophers, were in discussion regarding their unique view of life in 1933. They reduced their collective thoughts to writing and adopted the first Humanist Manifesto expressing the central points of their humanistic philosophy of life. That document was made more contemporaneously relevant with the adoption of a second version in 1973. This is the third version, adopted in 2003 by the American Humanist Association as the current guiding consensus statement of philosophic principles that are agree upon by most humanists:

Humanism is a progressive philosophy of life that, without supernaturalism, affirms our ability and responsibility to lead ethical lives of personal fulfillment that aspire to the greater good of humanity.

The lifestance of Humanism—guided by reason, inspired by compassion, and informed by experience—encourages us to live life well and fully. It evolved through the ages and continues to develop through the efforts of thoughtful people who recognize that values and ideals, however carefully wrought, are subject to change as our knowledge and understandings advance.

This document is part of an ongoing effort to manifest in clear and positive terms the conceptual boundaries of Humanism, not what we must believe but a consensus of what we do believe. It is in this sense that we affirm the following:

Knowledge of the world is derived by observation, experimentation, and rational analysis. Humanists find that science is the best method for determining this knowledge as well as for solving problems and developing beneficial technologies. We also recognize the value of new departures in thought, the arts, and inner experience—each subject to analysis by critical intelligence.

Humans are an integral part of nature, the result of unguided evolutionary change. Humanists recognize nature as self-existing. We accept our life as all and enough, distinguishing things as they are from things as we might wish or imagine them to be. We welcome the challenges of the future, and are drawn to and undaunted by the yet to be known.

Ethical values are derived from human need and interest as tested by experience. Humanists ground values in human welfare shaped by human circumstances, interests, and concerns and extended to the global ecosystem and beyond. We are committed to treating each person as having inherent worth and dignity, and to making informed choices in a context of freedom consonant with responsibility.

Life's fulfillment emerges from individual participation in the service of humane ideals. We aim for our fullest possible development and animate our lives with a deep sense of purpose, finding wonder and awe in the joys and beauties of human existence, its challenges and tragedies, and even in the inevitability and finality of death. Humanists rely on the rich heritage of human culture and the lifestance of Humanism to provide comfort in times of want and encouragement in times of plenty.

Humans are social by nature and find meaning in relationships. Humanists long for and strive toward a world of mutual care and concern, free of cruelty and its consequences, where differences are resolved cooperatively without resorting to violence. The joining of individuality with interdependence enriches our lives, encourages us to enrich the lives of others, and inspires hope of attaining peace, justice, and opportunity for all.

Working to benefit society maximizes individual happiness. Progressive cultures have worked to free humanity from the brutalities of mere survival and to reduce suffering, improve society, and develop global community. We seek to minimize the inequities of circumstance and ability, and we support a just distribution of nature's resources and the fruits of human effort so that as many as possible can enjoy a good life.

Humanists are concerned for the well being of all, are committed to diversity, and respect those of differing yet humane views. We work to uphold the equal enjoyment of human rights and civil liberties in an open, secular society and maintain it is a civic duty to participate in the democratic process and a planetary duty to protect nature's integrity, diversity, and beauty in a secure, sustainable manner.

Thus engaged in the flow of life, we aspire to this vision with the informed conviction that humanity has the ability to progress toward its highest ideals. The responsibility for our lives and the kind of world in which we live is ours and ours alone.

Bibliography and Suggested Reading

(The two books highlighted in bold are the most important sources for improving your own life.)

Buber, Martin, "I and Thou," (2nd ed.; R.G. Smith, translation; New York, Charles Scribners, 1958)

Buber, Martin, "The Knowledge of Man; A Philosophy of the Inter-human", (New York, Harper Torch books, 1965)

Goble, Frank, "The Third Force," (New York, Grossman Publishers, Inc., 1970)

Hoffman, Edward, "The Right To Be Human, a Biography of Abraham Maslow," (New York, McGraw-Hill, 1999)

Keirsey, David, "Please Understand Me II," (Del Mar, CA, Prometheus Nemesis Book Company, 1998)

Maslow, Abraham H., "The Further Reaches of Human Nature," (New York, The Viking Press, 1971) (New York, Penguin Books, 1976; Arkana, 1993)

Maslow, Abraham H., "Motivation and Personality," (New York, Harper Collins 1987)

Simpson, Lyle L. "Abraham Maslow's Purpose For Your Life," (Houston, *Essays on Humanism*, Humanists of Houston, Volume 11, 2002, now published by the American Humanist Association)

Simpson, Lyle L. "What is the Purpose For Your Life?" (Washington, *Essays on Humanism*, American Humanist Association, Volume 13, 2005)

Spong, John Shelby "Jesus for the Non-Religious," Harper-Collins e-books.

Tillich, Paul "Dynamics of Faith," (New York Harper Torchbooks, 1957)